THE WINES OF CHABLIS

1275

J -

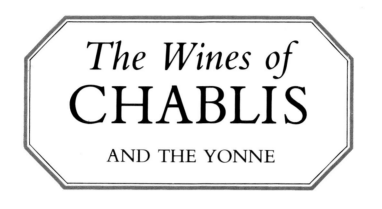

The Wines of
CHABLIS
AND THE YONNE

Rosemary George

Sotheby Publications
IN ASSOCIATION WITH
The Wine Appreciation Guild

© Rosemary George 1984
First published 1984 for
Sotheby Publications by
Philip Wilson Publishers Ltd,
Russell Chambers, Covent Garden,
London WC2E 8AA

Available to the USA book trade from
Harper and Row, Publishers, Inc
Keystone Industrial Park
Scranton
Pennsylvania 18512

Exclusive distribution to the wine trade
in the USA:
THE WINE APPRECIATION GUILD
155 Connecticut Street
San Francisco
California 94107
(415) 864–1202

ISBN 0 85667 179 7
Library of Congress Catalog Number 84-50544

Designed by Mary Osborne and Peter Ling
Phototypeset in Great Britain by Galleon Photosetting, Ipswich
Printed and bound in Singapore by Khai Wah Litho Pte Limited

CONTENTS

ACKNOWLEDGMENTS

This book would never have been written without the help of two friends. My thanks go to Martin Forde, who first introduced me to the delights of Chablis. It was his initial explanation of 'la situation chablisienne' that sowed the seeds of *The Wines of Chablis*, and his constructive reading of my first draft that has made this a much better book. Secondly, I must thank Shona Low for all her help and encouragement during my various visits to Chablis. I am very grateful to Peter Sichel, of Maison Sichel in Bordeaux, for allowing me to quote extensively from his invaluable vintage reports, to Jill Preston for helping me to unravel the intricacies of the geology of the area, and to Jenny Jenkins and Gabrielle Shaw for reading the text and checking the galleys. Last, but by no means least, *un grand merci* to all the growers of Chablis and its surrounding vineyards, who feature in the text and made this book possible by their willingness to discuss their work and share their wines with me.

Jim Chevallier deserves special thanks for giving up a weekend in November, when Chablis is cold and grey, to photograph growers in their even colder cellars. My thanks are also due to the following for permission to reproduce photographs: the Office de Tourisme de l'Yonne (the photographs were taken by J. C. Raby), Alain Geoffroy, Michel Laroche, Bichot et Compagnie, David Kitchen and the Library of the Masters of Wine at the Guildhall Library, London.

ROSEMARY GEORGE
January 1984

FOREWORD

The President of one of the most distinguished champagne houses and I were discussing export opportunities a year ago. 'What is it, do you think, that we are selling?' he asked. Before I could speak he gave the answer himself: 'Not the stuff in the bottle—*dreams!*'

The impact of advertising cannot be underestimated in creating and developing the reputations of fine wines. In order to sustain public curiosity in the great wines, such as Montrachet, Champagne, Yquem, Schloss Vollrads or Chablis, the producers have to present to the world, decade after decade, a judicious mixture of carefully selected information and myth (or 'dreams').

However, the publication of *The Wines of Chablis* succeeds not only by focusing attention on the wine but also by entirely altering its status in the wine world of the 1980s. Opinions will alter and people inside the wine trade, and out, will see what my small son calls 'Chabbers' in a new light.

During her stays in Chablis, researching diligently, rushing from one appointment to another (most often on a borrowed pushbike), Rosemary very quickly contributed to the existing local colour. Mademoiselle George has built up a fund of goodwill for the *rosbifs* as a species. It won't ever be reflected in preferential prices, but there will quite probably be especially friendly treatment for those strange animals from across the Channel.

I would hate to let pass without note two episodes in the five years I lived and worked in Chablis as a *négociant*.

The first vignette is about the coming together of two entirely different civilizations: the French and the Japanese. We were tasting one day with a group of Japanese, from a major importer in Tokyo, and my partner climbed a ladder with a pipette to draw off some Les Clos from a twenty-five hecto vat perched high up. One of the Japanese, astonished to see so small a vat, narrowed his eyes and exclaimed, 'Is that all there is!'

The second story illustrates the point made by Rosemary George that Chablis is *very* small and *very* quiet. Late one morning I was visited by a good friend and customer who runs an admirable carriage-trade wholesale business in New York. I suggested that a cup of coffee would be a good idea, so we left my office, crossed the deserted market square, and walked another fifty yards to the almost empty café. 'Ah hah,' said Barry, with a broad New Yorker's grin, 'I suppose this is what you call downtown Chablis!'

Chablis is not without its economic worries, even as this book goes to press. However, Rosemary George's knowledge and enthusiasm will help to develop and spread the reputation of Chablis in the coming years. You are hereby invited to share her enjoyment both in the glass and on the page.

MARTIN FORDE
Poinchy, January 1983

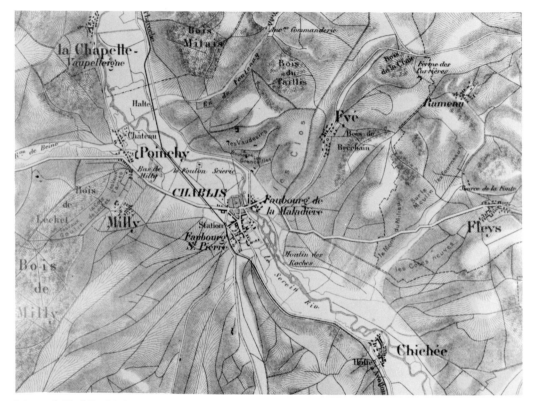

Map of Chablis (*Atlas Vinicole*, 1901)

INTRODUCTION

Setting the Scene

Why a book on Chablis? One grower did think it was a joke when I rang him to make an appointment to see him, 'parce que je fais un livre sur les vins de Chablis'. But why not? One of the most surprising aspects of Chablis is that so little has been written about it. It is one of the best-known wines, or certainly one of the best-known wine names in the English-speaking world (although not in France itself), and yet the last separate publication on the vineyards of Chablis, Albert Pic's *Le Vignoble de Chablis*, appeared as long ago as 1935.

Since then Chablis has never been allotted more than a chapter in a book on Burgundy, always the first or the last, depending on whether the author was travelling north or south. It is true that Chablis is part of Burgundy. It is commonly called 'La Porte d'Or de la Bourgogne' ('the Golden Gate of Burgundy') and it has been historically and commercially linked with Burgundy for centuries; yet in many respects Chablis is a very isolated, independent and individual vineyard area, more appropriately called by another infrequently used epithet: 'L'Ile Vineuse' ('the Wine Island'). Chablis is geographically closer to the vineyards of Champagne than to those of the Côte d'Or, but the contact between these two areas is negligible and although the *négociants* of Beaune play an important role in the commerce of Chablis abroad, they have made little impact on the character of the Chablis area. So the particular interest and attraction of Chablis is that of a very small, isolated vineyard, with its own traditions and idiosyncracies, as well as a huge reputation.

When I first visited Chablis in May 1981 Michel Poitout, Jean Durup's *chef de cave*, told me that one hundred years ago, before the phylloxera crisis, there were 40,000 hectares of vines in the Yonne. Today there are barely 3,000 hectares, of which Chablis itself accounts for a little more than half. So historical curiosity makes us ask, 'What happened?' It was amazing to discover that the *département* of the Yonne had been the prolific producer of *vins de comptoirs* (*vins ordinaires*) for the Parisian cafés and that its vineyards had included once-famous names such as Epineuil, La Côte St Jacques and Clos de la Chainette, which is now reduced to a tiny vineyard on the outskirts of Auxerre. Chablis itself survived the ravages of *phylloxera*, two world wars and rural depopulation—but only just. The adherence of its growers to the Chardonnay grape distinguished Chablis from the other white wines of the area, but the hard climatic vicissitudes, with years of devastating frost, were such as to deter even the most optimistic *vigneron*. The vineyards were so empty of vines that in the hard winter of 1956 people skied down the slopes of Les Clos, on what is now the source of one of Chablis' most distinguished wines and some of the most valuable land in the area.

It would be impossible to write a book about a wine without thoroughly enjoying that wine. I do not think I shall ever tire of Chablis: it defies description. The Chardonnay grape – grown on limestone and clay soil, the famous kimmeridgian – makes wines with flavour, complexity and depth. Young Chablis is pale straw-coloured, with a hint of green; it has dryness and bite, but is never harsh or tart. As it ages it develops the characteristic 'goût de la pierre à fusil', the hint of stony gunflint (a term traditionally used to describe fine Chablis), yet retains an underlying leafy grassiness. The Chardonnay grape makes the finest dry white wines in the world, wines that in Chablis are rivalled only by those of the Côte d'Or and which acquire with age an infinite variety of subtle nuances of flavour.

Within the single appellation of Chablis there are many different distinctive vineyards, including seven *grands crus* and eleven *premiers crus*, each with its own character and style. Chablis itself comes from twenty communes, and although these are concentrated within a very small area, there are differences in terrain, aspect and microclimate that contribute to the subtleties of flavour in the wines. Then there is the human element; each of the many growers and *négociants éleveurs* who make Chablis gives the wine something of himself, the element of individuality and difference of method or technique that sets it apart from his neighbours.

I love the wines of Chablis and I love the place and the people. This book is the result of six visits between May 1981 and November 1982, amounting to some two months spent in talking to the people and tasting their wines. Most of the growers respond to an enthusiastic audience and, once they have decided that you are '*sérieuse*', are delighted to air their views and share their wines with you. They are men of the land; their fathers, grandfathers and great-grandfathers were *vignerons* before them and their sons and grandsons will follow in their footsteps. With few exceptions their horizons are limited to the slopes

The market square of Chablis at the beginning of the century. A bomb destroyed many of the buildings in 1940. The photographer is standing in front of the Etoile restaurant

of the Chablis vineyards and they remain untouched by the events of the outside world.

Chablis is a provincial backwater, a sleepy country town, with nothing to distinguish it from any other town in rural France. It is very unassuming; the unobservant would not realize that they were in the heart of a famous vineyard. The signs with growers' names are unobtrusive; there is a large barrel at the entrance of the town on the road from Auxerre, but otherwise little evidence of a vinous community. Yet if you stand on the bridge crossing the Serein, you can see the slopes of the *grands crus*, the vineyards just beyond the edge of the town.

The Serein meanders gently through the town, which only comes to life at midday, when everyone is going home to lunch. The somnolence of the afternoon is sometimes shattered by the noise of the black-arrowed Mirage fighters, performing their trial flights from the air force base at Dijon. Chablis suffered from a stray German bomb in 1940; the old centre was completely destroyed and has been most

The old café of Chablis at the beginning of the century. There is a new café on the site, rebuilt after the bomb damage

unhappily replaced by the dull urban architecture typical of many French provincial towns. Around the Collégiale de Saint Martin, the parish church of Chablis, there are charming crooked cobbled streets and narrow alleyways. Chablis has two churches. The more important, the Collégiale Saint Martin, was built by the monks of the Abbey of Saint Martin de Tours, and is said to be a replica of the Cathedral of Sens. The south door is decorated with a wonderful collection of wrought-iron work and horseshoes, as thanks-offerings to Saint Martin, who was said not only to be the patron saint of drunkards, not inappropriately for a wine community, but also of horsemen. The other church, the original parish church of the Faubourg Saint Pierre, was nearly destroyed in the Revolution and is now surrounded by the cemetery. There are only two other buildings of major note: the Obédiencerie, a fifteenth-century house that belonged to the monks of Saint Martin and whose much older cellars are said to have sheltered his body; and Le Petit Pontigny, the only remaining property in the town of the monks of Pontigny nearby, which dates back to the twelfth century and is now used for the festive activities of the Piliers Chablisiens, the local wine brotherhood.

The whole place has an unhurried air about it and it is hard to believe that anything could disturb its calm. But, as everywhere in France, local politics are not far below the surface and there is endless intriguing about property, power and money.

The surrounding countryside is gently undulating, undramatic and restful. As well as vineyards, there are fields of corn and cherry-trees, cowslips in the hedgerows in April and fields of yellow rape in May. On the hilltops above the vineyards are woods of oak, juniper and pine.

The nearest town of any size is Auxerre, some twenty kilometres away. It is an attractive country town, with three churches towering above red russet roofs. The Cathedral of Saint Etienne, the Abbey of Saint Germain and the church of Saint Pierre dominate the town as you cross the bridge over the Yonne. There are narrow cobbled streets, timber-beamed houses from the sixteenth century and an old clock tower. As Monsieur Michelin would say, 'vaut le voyage'.

Each of the twenty villages of the Chablisien has its own character and charm. I stayed with English friends at Poinchy, in the pretty pink stone eighteenth-century château. The atmosphere was very conducive to thinking Chablis and drinking Chablis, the only hazard being the pony who one day mistook my notes for some tasty wistaria when I was working at the bottom of the garden! I covered the shortish distances between villages on a bicycle and for journeys further afield, and with steeper gradients, I borrowed a friend's 'deux–deuch' (2 cv Citroën).

'On mange bien à Chablis,' for good food goes with fine wine; the best *andouillettes* to be found anywhere in France come from the local charcuterie and can be eaten at Au Vrai Chablis across the square. The other restaurant and only hotel is the Etoile, with its sombre panelled dining-room and a wine list with some of the best that Chablis has to offer, to accompany local fish dishes in the tradition of the great chef, Monsieur Bergerand, who started the restaurant. There is a vineyard in the proprietor's family and Madame Roy is proud to recommend the production of their small parcel of Bougros. For those with a sweeter tooth, the local *duché* biscuits are not to be missed – the ideal accompaniment, not to Chablis, but to ratafia.

There is only one Chablis and it is in France, nowhere else. I wanted to take up cudgels for this wine, this place, these people, for the reason that some people climb Everest: because it's there!

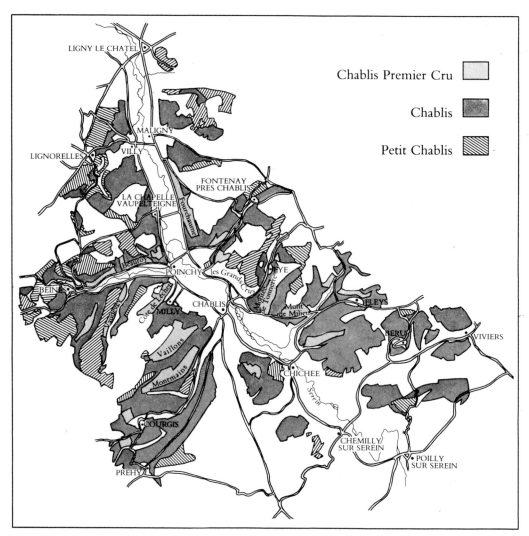

Chablis Premier Cru

Chablis

Petit Chablis

LIGNY LE CHATEL

MALIGNY

LIGNORELLES

VILLY

FONTENAY
PRES CHABLIS

LA CHAPELLE
VAUPELTEIGNE

Fourchaume

POINCHY

les Grands Crus

FYE

BEINES

Beauroy

Côte de Léchet

MILLY

CHABLIS

Montée de Tonnerre

Mont
de Milieu

FLEYS

BERU

VIVIERS

Vaillons

Montmains

Vaulorent

Serein

CHICHEE

COURGIS

CHEMILLY
SUR SEREIN

POILLY
SUR SEREIN

PREHY

Map of the vineyards of Chablis

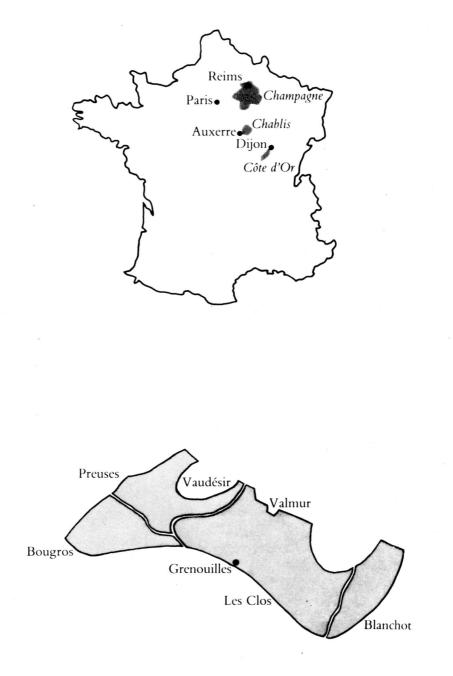

Detail, from the map of the vineyards of Chablis,
showing the *grand cru* properties

This is still a charcuterie shop – or, more precisely, a purveyor of *andouillettes*

1

HISTORY: FROM SAINT MARTIN DE TOURS UNTIL THE PRESENT DAY

The origins of the name Chablis are uncertain. Two suggestions have been put forward, but neither are entirely convincing. Chablis may be derived from a combination of two Celtic words, 'cab' ('house') and 'leya' ('wood') – that is, 'a house in the woods', but many towns are near woods, and there seems to be no reason why Chablis should be singled out. The other hypothesis derives from its situation on the River Serein. The first bridge across the Serein was not built until *c*. 1270. Before then travellers between Tonnerre and Auxerre had to use a boat with a cable to take them across the river. The Celtic word for a large cord is 'shable', which could easily have been altered to 'Chablis' over the years.

In Roman times the town was called Cableia, and although there may have been an early Celtic settlement on the site of the town, it was the Romans who, as in so many other parts of France, brought vines and viticulture to Chablis. However, when Domitian issued an edict in AD 92 forbidding the further planting of vines in Gaul and ordering that at least half the existing vines be torn up, viticulture had not yet reached the Yonne, and consequently its arrival there was delayed. Domitian's edict was not so much an attempt to protect Italian wines from the competition of French wines as a move to prevent land that was better suited to, and needed for, the production of grain from being converted into vineyards that would only produce inferior common wines.

The better vineyards of Gaul continued to flourish, despite Domitian's edict. By the time Probus became Emperor, the economic situation of Gaul had changed, and by reversing Domitian's edict in 276 and allowing vines to be grown throughout Gaul, Probus was able to open up the valleys of the Rivers Seine and Loire to viticulture. Some sources say that Probus even sent vines to Chablis; be that as it may, it is certain that he was ultimately responsible for the beginnings of wine production in the *département* of the Yonne.

Although the Romans introduced vines to Chablis, it was the mediaeval church that gave viticulture the impetus that it needed to establish itself as an essential part of the rural economy and landscape of the area. The first monastery in the region, a tiny cell, was founded in

Chablis in 510 and dedicated to Saint Loup; this monastery, together with the town of Chablis, was given to the monks of Saint Martin de Tours by Charles the Bald in 867. It happened in this way. Charles the Bald spent Christmas that year at the Abbey of Saint Germain in Auxerre. When his cousin, Hugo, the Abbot of Saint Martin de Tours, came to ask for a sanctuary for the relics of his monastery's founder (since the monks had been ejected from Tours by the Normans), the gift of the monastery of Saint Loup was the solution and the bones of Saint Martin were duly laid to rest there. The charter confirming this gift contains the first written mention of the name of Chablis. The exact site of the monastery of Saint Loup is unknown, although there is strong evidence that it may be where the Obédiencerie now stands.

The association between Chablis and Tours continued until the Revolution. The Abbot of Tours kept the title Abbot of Tours and Chablis, and in 1138 the construction of the Collégiale church of Saint Martin was begun under the initiative of Hugues of Merlignac (the former name of the nearby village of Maligny). The Collégiale is the parish church of Chablis today.

Although the monks of Saint Martin cultivated vines, it was the monks of Pontigny (about fifteen kilometres north of Chablis) who gave the greatest impetus to viticulture in Chablis. The austere white stone abbey of Pontigny is an offshoot of the Cistercian abbey of Cîteaux; it has provided refuge for two archbishops of Canterbury, Thomas à Becket and Stephen Langton, and contains the tomb of a third, Edmund Rich (or Saint Edmé, as he later became known), who died at Pontigny on his way to Rome. The Cistercian monks, in accordance with their traditions at Clos Vougeot in the Côte d'Or, created Clos La Vieille Plante at Pontigny. This vineyard, producing red wine, was still in existence in the early nineteenth century, for Jullien describes it in his classic study of 1822:[1] 'La Vieille Plante makes wine that combines the vigour and bouquet of Bordeaux with the other qualities of Burgundy. Aged, it astonishes gourmets.'

As this was the only vineyard of any note within the vicinity of the monastery, the monks wanted a larger vineyard in an area that was more suitable for the cultivation of vines, even if further from their monastery, and consequently they looked to Chablis. The monks of Saint Martin de Tours were already well established in Chablis and

---

[1] *Topographie de Tous les Vignobles Connus.* (Books listed in the Bibliography are cited by author and title only.)

would no doubt have resented any encroachments on their property and authority. Nevertheless, at some time during the twelfth century (either in 1118 or 1198) an agreement was concluded between the monks of Pontigny and those of Saint Martin de Tours. In return for an annual payment of ten muids of wine (a muid being an old measure for about 225 litres), the monks of Pontigny were allowed the use of thirty-six *arpents* (about twenty-two hectares) of land in Chablis, together with the use of the building that is still known as Le Petit Pontigny. There is doubt, however, about whether this agreement was made before or after a gift of land to the monks of Pontigny by Anseric II, Lord of Montréal and Seneschal of Burgundy; here again there is uncertainty about the date of the gift. Consequently, we cannot be sure whether Anseric's present heralded the beginnings of Pontigny's association with Chablis or was given after the agreement with the monks of Saint Martin de Tours. However, there is no doubt that it helped to establish the relationship between Pontigny and Chablis which was to continue until the French Revolution. The wine made at the vineyard was said to be worthy of the esteem of the monks and capable of long conservation. Le Petit Pontigny was run as an offshoot of the Pontigny vineyard, like Clos Vougeot and Cîteaux. The building still stands today and houses the Régie and a three-hundred-year-old wine press.

Already in the twelfth century the fame and reputation of Chablis was spreading in France. The wine's renown was sung in the twelfth-century fable 'La Bataille des Vins' and Fra Salimbène, who marvelled at the abundance of vines at Auxerre in the thirteenth century, also sang its praises: 'It is a white wine, sometimes golden, that has aroma and body, an exquisite and generous flavour and fills the heart with a happy confidence.'

By 1328 there were 500 *arpents* of vines out of 1,200 *arpents* of cultivated land in the commune of Chablis, belonging to 450 land-owners. One of the problems of viticulture was the same in the Middle Ages as today, shortage of labour, although not entirely for the same reasons, for in 1372 it is recorded that the vines produced only a little wine, 'because they remained partly uncultivated as a result of war and the scarcity of labourers'. 'Déjà,' says Albert Pic in 1935.

In the Middle Ages the River Serein formed the boundary between the lands of the counts of Champagne and the dukes of Burgundy, and so inevitably the development of the town of Chablis has been linked with both these *domaines* as well as with the court of France. During the early part of the Middle Ages Chablis was under the protection of the

Old postcard showing the gateway of the Porte Noël. Chablis has not changed much since the beginning of the century. Apart from the long-skirted ladies, this is a familiar view today

counts of Champagne. Then in 1367 it became a *prévôté royale* (royal provostship), with a coat of arms incorporating those of the King of France and those of Saint Martin de Tours. At the beginning of the fifteenth century the town was fortified with a system of towers and ramparts for which money was contributed from the commerce in wine. Fortifications were undoubtedly necessary, for northern France was continually disturbed by the unrest of the Hundred Years War and Chablis could not afford to ignore the events of the time. It was occupied by an English garrison after the defeat of Charles VII at Cravant in 1423 and Joan of Arc passed through Chablis in 1429. After the death of Charles the Bold, Duke of Burgundy, in 1477, Chablis was incorporated into the Duchy of Burgundy, an event which was to have an inestimable influence on the development of its viticulture and wines, for it was to align its wines with those of the Côte d'Or, rather than with those of Champagne.

After the strong impetus given to viticulture in Chablis by the monks of Pontigny and Saint Martin de Tours, it was the proximity of Chablis to Paris and the river systems of northern France that was the most significant factor in the growth of Chablis during the Middle Ages. In a time when journeys by road were hazardous and difficult, transport by river was of vital importance. The Serein itself was not navigable, but the Yonne was, and so, once the wine had covered the short distance by road to Auxerre, it was assured an easy journey to Paris – along the Yonne, into the Seine – and from Paris in to northern France, Picardy, Normandy and Flanders. The ease of transport was the crucial factor in the development of Chablis and the other wines of the Yonne during the Middle Ages and it explains why the wines of the Côte d'Or, which lacked a river system, remained unknown at that time.

The late fifteenth century, after the end of the Hundred Years War, was a period of great prosperity for the town, so much so that in 1478 Pierre Lerouge set up France's fifth printing press in Chablis. It produced two notable books: *Le Livre des Bonnes Moeurs* (1478) and *La Bréviaire d'Auxerre* (1483). After Pierre Lerouge's departure to Paris, other members of this family of printers worked in Chablis. Jehan Lerouge printed *Les Chartres d'Auxerre* and Guillaume Lerouge *Les Expositions des Evangiles* (1489). The population at that time numbered four thousand inhabitants; new houses were built and the vineyards flourished. Chablis had already acquired a reputation as the perfect accompaniment to oysters by the fifteenth century, when the poet Eustace Deschamps wrote:

> *Avec des huitres*
> *Que le Chablis est excellent;*
> *Je donnerai Fortune et Titres*
> *Pour m'enivrer de ce vin blanc*
> *Avec des huitres.*

('How excellent Chablis is with oysters. I will give up Fortune and Titles to get drunk on this white wine with oysters.')

By 1527 there were 700 vineyard owners, cultivating some 1,600 *arpents* (960 hectares) of land. By now the wines of Chablis were appreciated at the royal court of France and in 1529 there was an abortive attempt to make the Serein navigable, so that transport to the capital would be easier. However, the monks of Pontigny opposed the scheme, since the Serein crossed their land. During the sixteenth

21

century the wars of religion left their mark on Chablis: in 1568 the Huguenots besieged the town and burnt down the whole of the Faubourg Saint Pierre.

By the mid-seventeenth century the fame of Chablis had crossed the Channel, and the Earl of Bedford's cellars at Woburn contained stocks of the wine. In France, records of early vintages occasionally indicate that the problems encountered by growers today are by no means new: at the end of September 1692, for example, there was so much snow in the vineyards that the grapes froze, and in 1693 the vintage began on All Saints' Day (1 November) for the same reason.

In 1731 Louis XV forbade the planting of new vineyards in an attempt to remedy the prevailing shortage of grain, a measure reminiscent of Domitian's edict some seven centuries earlier. Two years later the population of Chablis were forced to ask for help and sustenance following five consecutive years of frost and failed vintages. In contrast, so much wine was made fifty years later, in 1781, that there was not enough room for it all in the cellars. Meanwhile, there had also been great vintages which enhanced the wine's reputation. Chanoine Gaudon wrote to Mme d'Epinay in 1759, 'My wine from Chablis this year has quality; when it is drunk, it embalms and enchants the throat and leaves the sweet flavour of *mousseron*.'[1]

Another poetic comment on the association of Chablis with oysters came from Le Chevalier de Piis at the Restoration Dinner of the Epicureans in the early nineteenth century:

> *Qui pourrait mettre en oublie*
> *Le limpide et Chablis,*
> *Qui joint à tant d'autres titres*
> *L'art de faire aimer les huitres.*

('Who can forget dry and limpid Chablis, which to many other virtues adds enrichment to the oyster.')

The French Revolution had a shattering effect on the equilibrium of the town of Chablis, as it had elsewhere in France, for it brought an end to the extensive monastic and ecclesiastical landownership. The vineyards of Pontigny, together with the property of the chapter of Saint Martin and of the various chapels of Chablis, were auctioned as *biens*

[1] A type of mushroom.

nationaux ('national property') and generally bought by local property owners, who tended either to be wine merchants or *commissionaires*, or members of the professions, such as the local lawyer and doctor. Three large landowners of the Ancien Régime managed to survive the Revolution, but at the beginning of the nineteenth century the vineyards of Chablis belonged to a small group of bourgeois property owners, most of whom were related by marriage. The rest of the vineyards were shared among the small farmers, who had a few acres of vines, along with their cows and wheat, and who also tended the vines of the bourgeois landowners. Although vines were important they were not, until very recently, the sole source of income; polyculture was the norm.

The ownership of a wine press was of considerable significance, for access to a press was vital if any benefit was to be obtained from owning vines. At the beginning of the nineteenth century there were 26 presses, owned by 22 families for 870 hectares of vines. The many small *vignerons* who did not own a press had to pay for the use of one, or resort to the more traditional method of pressing their grapes by foot.

Meanwhile, in England, Chablis had continued to make headway. The first white Burgundy to appear at a Christie's sale was a Chablis (catalogued as Chablet), in 1770. In his 'General Instructions for the Choice of Wines and Spirituous Liquors Dedicated to His Royal Highness, the Prince of Wales' (the future George IV), Dr McBride wrote in 1793 that 'the vin de Chable is a light pleasant wine and not unwholesome to be used at table instead of beer'. This is not as flattering as earlier eulogies, and history does not relate whether the Prince Regent forswore beer for Chablis; but it does show that Chablis was becoming one of the better known French wines in England. During the nineteenth century we find an allusion to Chablis by an English poet, Robert Browning:

> *Then I went indoor, brought out a loaf*
> *Half a cheese and a bottle of Chablis,*
> *Lay on the grass and forgot the oaf,*
> *Over a jolly chapter of Rabelais.*

In France the Franco-Prussian War was the next major upheaval to affect Chablis. In 1870 the town was ransomed by the Prussians as a reprisal for the death of a Prussian sub-lieutenant. Forty thousand francs had to be raised to secure the lives of the four hostages: Monsieur

Rathier (the mayor), Dubau (the *curé*), and Messieurs Depaquit and Pic (members of notable wine families).

The one great asset of Chablis and the surrounding vineyards of the Yonne was their proximity to Paris. As I have mentioned, although the Serein itself was not navigable, the Yonne was (except occasionally during the summer months), and wine was easily transported to Paris by river. In the late nineteenth century the railways took over, and communications with the capital improved enormously with the building of a railway line from Laroche Migennes to L'Isle-Angély in 1886. Not only Chablis, but even the tiny hamlet of Poinchy, had railway stations until 1952. (Stephen Gwynn[1] praises the Chablis of the station buffet at Laroche; I have only ever had the beer!) With the advent of the railway the majority of the surrounding villages succumbed to the temptation of providing the capital with cheap *vins de comptoir* for its cafés. High-yielding grape varieties such as the Plante Verte mentioned by Cavoleau (which was probably the present-day Sacy and was also called the Essert), and the Damery and Hivernage (which have now disappeared), were widely planted to supply the capital with light and undistinguished everyday drinking wines.

But the advantages of proximity to Paris were severely mitigated by three disasters which struck the vineyards of Chablis and the Yonne in the second half of the nineteenth century. These were *oidium*, phylloxera and (for purely commercial reasons) the railways, which benefited not only the growers of the area but their competitors elsewhere.

Powdery mildew, more commonly called *oidium*, first appeared in the Chablisien in 1886. Albert Pic records that the vines lost their leaves prematurely and that the resulting wine was barely passable in quantity and quality. Fortunately a cure was already known; the dusting of the vines with sulphur had already been proved effective in keeping the vines healthy, and was now used to deal with *oidium*.

Phylloxera was to prove a much more serious threat. The devastating louse that attacked the roots of the European vines was first found in a greenhouse in Hammersmith in 1863. It had been brought to Europe on some vine cuttings sent from the United States. Shortly afterwards it was found in the vineyards of southern France, but did not reach the Chablisien until 1887. The effect was to be disastrous. However, according to Albert Pic, the blight was slow to take hold initially. Indeed, at the very beginnings of the outbreak it can even be said that

[1] *Burgundy.*

The old-fashioned and laborious technique of spraying the vines with sulphur

Chablis benefited, for, since it was the vineyards of the Midi that were first attacked, those of the Yonne were able to continue supplying the capital with the cheap wines it required, without the threat of competition from the south (a subject to which I shall return in a moment).

Chablis, then, had the advantage of experience acquired in the earlier affected areas. But when the very hot summer of 1893 caused a population explosion of the louse, which rapidly spread throughout the vineyards, its growers still adopted some of the far-fetched, ineffective remedies which had been used in other areas. Albert Pic recalls a certain vaccine that was applied to the vines where they had been pruned, and which was supposed to give them renewed vigour, as well as killing the phylloxera louse. Needless to say, it did neither. However, a treatment of carbon bisulphide, applied regularly in the spring and autumn, succeeded in prolonging the life of some of the old French vines until about 1906. The only effective remedy lay in the grafting of European vines onto American rootstock, which was being done in some parts of France by the mid-1880s. The first such plantings took place in Chablis after the outbreak in 1897, and the first results were vintaged in 1902. Although this method became accepted as the only solution to the phylloxera crisis, the cost of replanting the vineyards was enormous and many growers were unable to meet it.

The third catastrophe was brought about indirectly by the railways, whose arrival, although initially highly beneficial to Chablis, was disastrous in the long term. The completion of the Paris–Lyon–Marseilles railway line in 1856 brought the cheap wines of the Midi within easy reach of Parisians, and once the remedy to phylloxera had been found, the wines of the Yonne lost their advantageous position and were unable to compete with those of the Midi on price alone. The vineyards of the Yonne could never escape from the vicissitudes of their northern climate; they were constantly the victims of frost and could not regularly produce the high yields of the warm south. Thus the pattern was set for a long period of decline in the vineyard area of the Yonne. The vineyards that were replanted after the phylloxera outbreak were those which produced wines of quality, meriting conservation – that is, the vineyards around the town of Chablis itself. The vineyards of villages like Poilly, Yrouerre, Chemilly and Collan disappeared; Sacy and Joux-la-Ville replaced their vines with plantations of pine-trees.

What phylloxera, and competition from the Midi, had begun, the labour shortages of the First World War and subsequent rural de-population continued. Even more vineyards fell into disuse after 1914, when the labour forces of entire villages were conscripted and the horses were requisitioned, so that only the women and old people were left to carry on the unequal struggle of maintaining the land and the vineyards. Once the war was over, the lure of work in the capital, with a regular weekly wage – an easy living, compared to the hard and often discouraging existence of a farmer and *vigneron* – hastened the rural exodus. Yet more vineyards ceased to be used; those which were subsequently not included in the delimitation of Chablis, and even those on well favoured (if frost-prone) sites, were left long unplanted. The vineyards of Chablis reached their nadir just after the Second

World War, when less than five hundred hectares were left planted with vines.

Fortunately the tide turned. The arrival of the tractor and the introduction of effective measures of frost prevention at the beginning of the 1960s not only transformed the viability of the vineyards, but resulted in the dramatic increase in the vineyard area discussed in my next chapter.

The Vineyards of Chablis: their Names and their Wines

The origins of the names of the vineyards are uncertain; some *climats* were mentioned by name as early as the twelfth century, and certainly by the beginning of the nineteenth there were many recognized sites, a number of which form part of the present classification of *grands* and *premiers crus*. I give below such information as I have been able to assemble about the individual vineyards, from the early nineteenth century onwards. I am indebted to M. Robert Fèvre – one of the great characters of Chablis – for providing me with details of the origins of the vineyards' names.[1]

The vineyard named Les Lys was perhaps owned by the royal prevost and takes its name from the royal coat of arms. Les Clos was possibly a walled vineyard at one time. Montée de Tonnerre recalls the old road to Tonnerre that went up a steep hill alongside the vineyards. The name Blanchot refers to the particularly white terrain of the vineyard, and Grenouille is the nearest vineyard to the Serein, where no doubt the workers could hear the frogs. (Michel Rémon remembers living as a child in a house overlooking the Serein and being kept awake by the 'bruit infernal' of the frogs.

By the beginning of the nineteenth century the reputation of Chablis was established, and it was recognized, both in France and abroad, as a white wine of considerable quality. In 1822 Jullien[2] places it after the white wines of Tonnerre, saying that its best wines are nearly as good as Meursault: 'They are strong without being too heady, have body, finesse and a pleasant flavour.' The best is 'Le Clos, whose wine was

---

[1] M. Robert Fèvre (no relation to William Fèvre, of Domaine de la Maladière) – local historian and raconteur – left school at the age of fourteen in 1924 to learn the work of a *vigneron* from his grandfather. He has seen many changes in the vineyards of Chablis.
[2] Op cit.

Robert Fèvre, the local historian and a fountain of information on Chablis past and present

strong and a little hard the first year, becoming very pleasant after eighteen months and keeping perfectly'. Of Valmur and Grenouilles he writes, 'ils donnent des vins, qui en primeur ont plus de douceur et délicatesse que ceux du Clos, mais lorsqu'ils ont perdu cette qualité, nommée dans le commerce *moustille*, ils sont moins spiritueux et ne se conservent pas aussi longtemps.' ('They make wines which, when young, are softer and more delicate than those of Le Clos, but when they have lost this quality, called *moustille* in the trade, they are not so strong and do not keep for so long.') Finally Vaudésir, Bouguereau (as Bougros was and can still be called) and Mont de Milieu are also mentioned in the first category as vineyards 'which give very elegant wines, with the most perfect clarity.' To attain their quality they should be kept in *tonneau* for two years and bottled for one year, before they are ready; but after this they will keep for a long time.

In his second category Jullien places La Côte Delchet at Milly (now known as Côte de Léchet), Fourchaume, Troëme, Vaucompin (now known as Vaucoupin), Blanchot and Fontenay. These wines were apparently slightly different from those in the first category, usually belonging to Chablis producers and often mixed with their other better wines. Also in the second category we find Chapelot, Vauvilieu, Preuses, Vaulorent, Vosgros and the bottom slopes of Le Clos – again, some familiar, and some unfamiliar, names among today's *grands* and *premiers crus.*

In his third category Jullien lists a number of villages: some of these are included among the nineteen other communes now entitled to the appellation of Chablis; others either now produce only a simple white Burgundy, or no wine at all. Viviers, Béru and Fleys 'give ordinary wines, pleasant and spirituous'; Roffey, Serigny, Tissey, Vézannes, Bernouil and several others make good wines to keep. Milly, Maligny, Poinchy, Villy, Chichée, Ligny-le-Châtel, Poilly, Chemilly, Courgy 'also give ordinary wines and common wines among which you can find some quite good ones'.

In 1827 another writer on wine, J. A. Cavoleau,[1] sings the praises of the Pineau Blanc grape in Chablis, when it is not mixed with any other varieties: 'it is not found anywhere better than at Chablis', where it produces wine with the distinctive 'goût de la pierre à fusil'. This is the first mention of 'gunflint', which has become the standard term with which to describe fine Chablis. Cavoleau's second category consists of wines made from Pineau Blanc or Plante Verte grown either in Chablis itself or in other parts of the area, where they are also called Chablis. The third category of wines was made from Plante Verte, grown in a bad aspect and soil. Cyrus Redding, the English wine-writer of the early nineteenth century, reiterates Cavoleau's remarks.[2]

---

[1] *Oenologie Française.*
[2] *A History and Description of Modern Wines.*

In a study published in 1863,[1] Dr Jules Guyot says that 'the wines of Chablis are among the best white wines of France' after Meursault. He praises them in lyrical terms: 'Strong, but without effect, they have body, finesse and a charming flavour; their whiteness and limpidity are remarkable. But they distinguish themselves above all for their hygienic and digestive qualities and for the benevolent and lucid liveliness that they give to the mind. In spite of the great reputation that they rightly enjoy and have done for a long time, in my opinion their real value is even higher than their renown.'

Here Guyot is describing the wines that were produced on the best hillsides around the town of Chablis, but not all Chablis was as fine as these. Before the introduction of the *appellation contrôlée* laws in 1938 the name of Chablis was used to describe the white wine produced in some eighty-four villages in the Yonne between Pontigny and Joux-la-Ville, irrespective of grape variety, character and quality. As Victor Rendu comments in 1857,[2] the neighbouring growers took advantage of the proximity and similar character of their wines to sell them under the name of Chablis. Moreover, wine from the area was bought by the Champagne houses of Epernay and Reims. This was a practice that was to continue until the area of Champagne was defined at the beginning of the twentieth century. Indeed, when, between 1908 and 1911, the growers of the Aube wished to send delegates to Paris to argue their claim that they should be included in the area of Champagne, they asked the growers of Chablis for their support and help. This was refused, for despite their proximity to the vineyards of Champagne, the growers of Chablis considered themselves to be a part of Burgundy, not of Champagne.

There is so much confusion regarding varieties of grape (a subject discussed more fully in Chapter 3) that it is virtually impossible to distinguish between the three varieties that are most commonly referred to in connection with Chablis in the nineteenth century. Jullien and Cavoleau both mention Pineau Blanc (or Pinot Blanc as we now call it), as the best white grape of the area, whereas for Dr Guyot the grape of Chablis is 'the unique and traditional plant, the Morillon Blanc'. He says that the oenologist Odart has correctly classified it in the Pinot family, but that it is not the same as Pinot Blanc or Chardenet (Chardonnay), also known as the Beaunois in the Chablisien, perhaps

---

[1] *Etude des Vignobles de France.*
[2] *Ampelographie Française.*

Vineyard in the Chablis hills, showing the training of vines

because it was introduced to the area from Beaune. By the time of the introduction of the *appellation contrôlée* laws Chardonnay was accepted as the only variety of grape capable of producing Chablis; the Morillon Blanc had disappeared from common usage and the Pinot Blanc was accepted as a separate variety, being no longer grown in the Yonne. However, according to a modern authority, Pierre Galet,[1] both the Morillon Blanc and the Pinot Blanc are synonyms of the Chardonnay. One thing is certain: it was the adherence of the Chablis growers to the finest grape variety – namely, Chardonnay – that ensured the survival

[1] *Cépages et Vignobles de France.*

of Chablis during the decline of the vineyards of the Yonne during the later part of the nineteenth century.

The ownership of the vineyards remained with the same families, with little change, throughout the nineteenth century. These were families such as Rathier, Mignard, Hochet, Thomessin and so on, who had benefited from the sale of the *biens nationaux* after the Revolution. With the reconstitution of the vineyards after the phylloxera crisis there was some infiltration of people from outside the region, and after the Second World War the ownership of the vineyards became less concentrated in the same small group of families. Since the return of prosperity to the vineyards in the 1960s the rural exodus has been reversed, and people whose families had once left the region have been returning. There has also been a marked consolidation in the vineyard holdings. In 1955 an average holding was about two hectares, which was often split into several tiny parcels. An aerial photograph of Chablis taken in the 1950s shows the vineyards in patchwork strips, a couple of rows of vines adjoining a small parcel of wheat – or, even more likely, a patch of fallow or wasteland. The complicated French laws of inheritance were responsible for this multiplicity of tiny holdings; one man, for example, needed 300 documents to give to a holding of 240 hectares of farmland and vines some semblance of organization. Even today the more traditional *vignerons* will say that they were 'dans la vigne', as though they had been working on a single row of vines.

The twentieth century has also seen the development of the *appellation contrôlée* regulations, referred to above, which have helped Chablis to establish its position as the finest white wine of the Yonne. However, as the following chapter relates, their introduction, together with the expansion of the vineyards, has not been without its problems and controversy.

The steep slopes of the *grand cru* vineyards

2
THE DELIMITATION OF THE VINEYARDS: DEFINITION AND EXPANSION

An appreciation of the need to protect the quality of a wine goes back to the Middle Ages. Philippe le Hardi, Duke of Burgundy, ordered the uprooting of the gamay vine from the vineyards of Dijon, Beaune and Chalon in 1395. The 'très mauvais et très déloyaux plant nommé gamay' was banned from these vineyards on account of its poor quality. Perhaps the first delimitation of an area of production came in an enactment of Charles VI in 1416, which was confirmed by François I in 1527, and stated that 'all sorts of wines harvested above the bridge at Sens, as much those of the Auxerrois as those of the Beaunois . . . which travel on the Yonne river shall be called Vins de Bourgogne'.

During the nineteenth century over eighty villages sold their wine, made from numerous different grape varieties, under the umbrella of Chablis. Worse still, there is evidence that in 1898 a *négociant* from Chablis bought considerable quantities of 'vin blanc de la Manche [La Mancha], 12° à raison de 30 francs l'hectolitre nu pris à Cette [Sète]'. Not surprisingly there is no mention of any subsequent sale of Spanish wine. The need for a definition of the Chablis vineyards was clearly vital; if the reputation of the wines produced in them was·to be preserved, it was essential to distinguish these from the wines produced in neighbouring villages.

The beginnings of a movement towards a delimitation of the vineyards and the protection of the name of Chablis came in 1900, when the phylloxera crisis was at its height. Seventy-nine growers formed a union with the object, in the words of its president, 'of guaranteeing the authenticity of the wines and grouping all the vineyard proprietors together in order to promote the sale of their products'. A register placed 'à la disposition de tous les acheteurs . . . contient la nomenclature et le classement par ordre alphabétique au point de vue oenologique, de toutes les côtes productives de vin blanc'. ('At the disposal of all the buyers . . . contains the name and classification in alphabetical order, from the oenological point of view, of all the slopes producing white wine'.) The origin of the wine was to be guaranteed by a wax seal on each *feuillette*. This association of growers had no legal backing and was consequently powerless and ineffective, but it was significant as an early attempt to protect the quality and origins of Chablis.

The next attempt came in 1908 with the formation of a 'Union des Propriétaires-Vignerons de Chablis'. Again, it was without legal recourse, but a letter from the President, Monsieur Long Depaquit, illustrates the situation: 'Le nom de Chablis, jadis universellement connu et estimé, sert aujourd'hui de pavillon à des vins blancs de toute provenance. Notre récolte annuelle est en moyenne de quinze mille hectolitres de vin et il se vend tous les ans, soit en France, soit à l'étranger un million d'hectolitres du vin blanc de Chablis.' ('The name of Chablis, once universally known and respected, serves today as a flagship for white wines of all origins. Our annual harvest is on average fifteen thousand hectolitres and a million hectolitres of wine are sold every year, in both France and abroad, under the name of Chablis.') The general intention was to keep the name of Chablis for the production of the growers of Chablis itself, who between them owned most of the vineyards on the right bank of the Serein, between Fourchaume and Mont de Milieu. Sometimes the term 'Environs de Chablis' could be found. The application of the name 'Chablis' to a wine from outside the area usually resulted in a higher price and, consequently, numerous attempts at fraud.

This second union did manage to prevent two growers from surrounding villages from selling their wine as Chablis Viviers and Chablis Beines, but otherwise it was to remain more or less powerless for over ten years, until a law was passed in 1919 by the French legislative assembly, laying down the principles of *appellation d'origine* and their conformity to 'les usages locaux, loyaux et constants'. The unions of each region were given the authority to enable them to take legal action to defend their rights. The Union des Propriétaires-Vignerons de Chablis accordingly amended its statute to state that it was formed 'pour empêcher la fraude et défendre les grands crus' ('to prevent fraud and protect the grands crus').

Following this, a commission of growers and *négociants* was set up under the auspices of the Prefect, and, as a result, the following measures were agreed on 2 August 1919:

1 The *grands crus* were delimited.
2 Only wines made from Pinot Chardonnay, commonly called Beaunois, harvested in Chablis and the adjoining communes of Fontenay-près-Chablis, Fyé, Milly, Poinchy, Chichée, Courgis,

Fleys (with Mont de Milieu), La Chapelle Vaupelteigne (*climat* of Fourchaume) and Beines (*climat* of Troême) had the right to the appellation of Chablis.

3 The white wines from the same area, but from grape varieties other than the Beaunois, should be called Petit Chablis.

However, a few days later, on 15 August, the Commission of the Yonne independently devised a much wider delimitation. It accorded the appellation of Chablis to all wines made from the Beaunois in the canton of Chablis and the adjoining cantons of Auxerre, Vermenton, Noyers and Coulanges-la-Vineuse – in other words, to almost the entire production of wine made from the Chardonnay grape in the Yonne.

The growers of Chablis appealed against this decision in January 1920 before the Commission of Burgundy, which thereupon fixed three appellations:

1 Grands Vins de Chablis (the *grands crus* already defined in August 1919).

2 Chablis Village Superieur (for wines made from Chardonnay in the other communes of the canton of Chablis (as agreed in 1919; see above) and the communes of Ligny-le-Châtel, Lignorelles, Maligny, Villy, Beines, Viviers and Chemilly-sur-Serein).

3 Chablis Village (for all the other white wines produced in these communes).

This classification appeared to obtain the support of many of the growers of Chablis and the surrounding villages, but was never strictly applied, as no legislation confirmed the decision. Nevertheless, the law of 1919, creating the concept of 'les usages locaux, loyaux et constants' marked the beginning of a series of law suits that were to result in a more formal delimitation of the area of Chablis. A case was fought against the growers of Lignorelles, Villy and Montigny-la-Resle to forbid them from selling their wine under the appellation of Chablis or Bourgogne Chablis. The judgement of December 1920 considered the subjects of grape variety, terrain, aspect and cultivation methods, observing notably that 'the wines of the region properly called Chablis come from a soil made up of kimmeridgian marl'. It forbade these three communes to use the name Chablis on the grounds that their wines were not produced from the same soil as was Chablis. They were free to use the term Chablis Village or Chablis Village Supérieur, as suggested by the Commission de Bourgogne. This was the first mention of the famous kimmeridgian soil in relation to the quality of Chablis in a legislative decision.

The growers of Chablis began to fear that an element of ambiguity would arise from the terms Chablis Village and Chablis Village Supérieur, and they therefore sought to forbid the use of the word Chablis for all wines whose methods of production were not identical to those of Chablis itself. An agreement was reached which was ratified by the Tribunal de Tonnerre in 1923. The term Chablis Village was abandoned; the appellation of Chablis was limited to wine produced from the Chardonnay grape on kimmeridgian soil, and the term Petit Chablis was introduced to cover all wine produced from Chardonnay on other soil. This was accepted by the growers of Maligny, La Chapelle Vaupelteigne, Beines, Ligny-le-Châtel, Béru, Lignorelles and Villy. All that remained to be done was to define the limits of the kimmeridgian soil, and, with that, the area of the appellation of Chablis would have been settled. But this was not to be.

For the significance and importance of the grape variety, of the contribution of the Chardonnay to the essential character of Chablis, was thrown into doubt by a dispute between the growers of Chitry and those of Chablis. Between 1925 and 1930 the Sacy grape had assumed such importance in the vineyards in relation to the Chardonnay that the growers of Chablis thought it useless to attempt to protect their area of production if they could not also safeguard the grape variety. Fortunately the *loi Capus*, passed in 1927, confirmed the importance of the grape variety among 'les usages locaux, loyaux et constants'. Consequently an agreement was made between the growers of Chablis and the Syndicat du Commerce en Gros des Vins de l'Yonne which was ratified by the Tribunal d'Auxerre in 1929. It contained three points:

1 The vineyard of Chablis consists of the eighteen communes originally mentioned, together with Poilly-sur-Serein and Collan (for the hamlet of Rameau).
2 Only wine made from Pinot Chardonnay in these communes is to have the right to the appellation of Chablis.
3 Wines from other grape varieties from the twenty communes, as well as from Chitry, can be given the appellation Bourgogne des Environs de Chablis.

The terms Chablis Village Supérieur, Chablis Village and Petit Chablis were suppressed. No mention was made of soil – an omission that was to beset the history of the appellation for the next half-century.

In the light of this decision, Albert Pic defined the vineyards of Chablis in 1935 and listed the *crus*, dividing them into four categories, as follows:[1]

Têtes premiers crus
Blanchot   Grenouilles
Les Clos   Vaudésir
Valmur

Premiers crus
Mont de Milieu   Preuses
Chapelot   Fourchaume (commencement de la côte)
Montée de Tonnerre   Vaulorent (à droit seulement)

Deuxièmes crus
Les Forêts   Séchet
Montmains   Les Epinottes
Beugnon   Vaucoupin
Vaillons   Côte de Léchet
Mélinots   Beauroy
Roncières   Troëmes
Les Lys   Côte de Fontenay

Troisièmes crus
All the slopes with a less favourable aspect.

The names of the *premiers* and *deuxièmes crus* include the principal names of today's *grands* and *premiers crus*. The twenty communes of Chablis are then listed and Bourgogne des Environs de Chablis is defined according to the judgement of the Tribunal d'Auxerre.

At the time that Albert Pic was writing the French government enacted a decision not to leave the responsibility of defining the conditions of the production of *vins d'appellation* to local judgements, but to create a specialized national Comité National d'Appellations d'Origine (CNAO) that was later to become the Institut National des Appellations d'Origine (INAO). This decision was prompted by a general stagnation in the wine trade during the early 1930s, as a result of the world economic crisis.

[1] Whether the name of a vineyard is in the singular or the plural, and whether or not it is preceded by the definite article, is a matter which depends on the individual grower's preference.

Accordingly a government decree prepared by the CNAO in January 1938 defined the appellation of Chablis. It confirmed the 1923 rulings regarding the soil of the vineyards and assumed that the 1929 tribunal merely clarified the question of the grape variety. So Chablis was to be the production of the Chardonnay grape, grown on kimmeridgian soil in the twenty communes. Again, all that was now needed was to define the extent of the vineyards on kimmeridgian soil, but this proved to be easier said than done.

Fifteen years earlier the task had been undertaken by the commission of experts appointed after the decision of the Tribunal de Tonnerre. Except in the communes of Maligny, Villy and Lignorelles, to the north of Chablis, the kimmeridgian soil was very apparent and conformed more or less to the plantings of Chardonnay. The disagreements resulted from the attempts to delimit the kimmeridgian soil in these three communes. The experts failed to agree among themselves. Some argued that the other soil of these communes, portlandian, was so similar to kimmeridgian as to be identical with it. Kimmeridgian and portlandian are both sedimentary soils and it is indeed very difficult to distinguish between them. There is no decisive geological fault which divides them – merely a gradual progression from one to the other. But the CNAO refused to accept that the two soils were similar. An agreement was never reached and the way was left open for further disputes.

The second problem was that of the Chardonnay grown on soil that could not in any way be accepted as kimmeridgian. This involved one hundred hectares of vines in the communes of Lignorelles, Villy and Maligny which were excluded from the appellation of Chablis in the plans of delimitation of 1943. Instead of perhaps creating a separate appellation, such as Lignorelles, the INAO (as the CNAO had by now become) decided to call this area (which consisted mainly of portlandian soil) Petit Chablis and, under a decree of January 1944, a term that had been forbidden in 1929 came back into existence again. To make matters worse, the area of Petit Chablis was never precisely delimited, so that growers in adjoining areas came gradually to use the name and all kinds of malpractices resulted. The abolition in April 1942 of the appellation Bourgogne des Environs de Chablis had done nothing to ease the situation.

A deluge of appeals followed the formation of the appellation of Petit Chablis. The INAO stalled for fifteen years over these claims. It was only in 1956 that a new committee of experts was appointed to reconsider the delimitation of Chablis. As a result, in 1960 the area of Chablis was extended by five hundred hectares, of which only fifty were already planted with vines. The decision met with general approval: it conformed to the spirit of the 1938 decree. None of the portlandian plateaus were included in the new delimitation and the modification satisfied the claimants in the northern part of the vineyard. The year 1960 also marked the creation of a *syndicat*, or union, for the growers of the vineyard of Chablis. It was to become a significant organization in representing the views of the growers, and, as in other wine areas, the *syndicat* plays an important role in decisions affecting the vineyard and in advising the INAO on matters such as vintage dates, *labellisation* tastings and so on.

The early 1960s were a period of consolidation. The vineyards were gradually expanding and, with the introduction of anti-frost measures, the growers were assured a certain security of livelihood. In January 1967 the *premiers crus* vineyards were classified and the nomenclature was simplified at the same time, so that twenty-four original names were reduced to eleven *premiers crus*. The main reason for this measure was a need to facilitate the commercialization of the *premiers crus*; a grower's holdings were often divided into many small parcels in different *climats*, with none producing enough wine to make it worth while to sell the wine of each plot separately. Often the wine was simply blended together and sold as Chablis Premier Cru. Also some of the vineyard names were totally unknown. From 1967 a grower could have a choice; he could, for instance, use the all-encompassing name of Fourchaume for the wine of three separate plots of vines, or he could sell each of them separately as Fourchaume, l'Homme Mort and Vaulorent.

The classification of 1967 stands as follows, with the main name followed by the smaller alternatives:

Fourchaume: Fourchaume, Vaupulent, Côte de Fontenay, Vaulorent, L'Homme Mort

Montée de Tonnerre: Montée de Tonnerre, Chapelot, Pied d'Aloup

Mont de Milieu

Vaucoupin (or Vaucoupain)

Les Fourneaux: Les Fourneaux, Morein, Côte des Près-Girots

Beauroy: Beauroy, Troesmes (or Troême)

Côte de Léchet

Vaillons: Vaillons, Châtains, Séchet (or Séché), Beugnon, Les Lys

Mélinots: Mélinots, Roncières, Les Epinottes

Montmains: Montmains, Forêts, Butteaux

Vosgros: Vosgros, Vaugiraut

The *grands crus*, which have remained unchanged since the introduction of the appellation in 1938, are as follows, together with their area in hectares:

Blanchot	11.65	Valmur	13.20
Preuses	11.10	Vaudésir	16.19
Bougros	15.85	Les Clos	25.81
Grenouilles	9.68		

As explained on p. 91, La Moutonne consists of 2.35 hectares of the vineyards of Preuses and Vaudésir.

This summary of the definition of Chablis has concentrated on the delimitation of the area of the vineyard, but the *appellation contrôlée* regulations not only define the area of production, but also cover the grape variety, permitted yields, alcohol levels and methods of cultivation and vinification. Originally *grand cru* Chablis could not exceed a yield of thirty-five hectolitres per hectare, and other Chablis forty hectolitres per hectare. However, since 1974 the annual yield, or *rendement de base*, has been fixed every year (taking into account the particular conditions of the year), and an additional twenty per cent. Plafonde Limite de Classement (PLC) is permitted by the INAO, provided that the wine is of the required standard. Any excess is declassified into *vin de table* (table wine); alternatively, the grower must have it distilled. Minimum alcohol levels must also be reached, with the assistance of chaptalization (see p. 66) if necessary. These levels are 11° for *grands crus*, 10.5° for *premiers crus*, 10° for simple Chablis[1] and 9.5° for Petit Chablis. In practice, however, higher levels are preferred.

The latest official measure regarding the appellation of Chablis was taken in 1978, following a new examination of the area of Chablis: 'A study that has taken into account all the factors, notably the pedological and climatic factors, and not just the geological factors'.[2] This study resulted in a further revision and expansion of the area of the vineyards. The INAO decided to extend the vineyards of Chablis and, in doing so,

[1] Not a pejorative term, this is used here to distinguish Chablis of the basic appellation from *grand cru* or *premier cru* Chablis.

[2] Letter from the INAO.

both to relegate the significance of kimmeridgian soil and to consider the importance of micro-climate and aspect in assessing the vineyards. Consequently the area of Chablis has been extended, some vineyards of Petit Chablis have been reclassified as Chablis and there is now an enormous potential for increasing the production of simple Chablis. Petit Chablis is not only being reduced in area but is being precisely delimited for the first time. The area of the *grands crus* has long been accepted without dispute, and remains unchanged. However, new areas of *premiers crus* vineyards have been proposed, based on the similarity of these areas to those of already recognized *premiers crus*. Although the exact zone of the *premiers crus* has not yet been redefined by the INAO, one new *premier cru* (Vaudevey, in the commune of Beines) will come into existence. It was planted in 1978 and the first assessment of its quality was made in 1983.

These measures of expansion have not met with the agreement of by any means all the growers. Since the early 1970s, when the move to expand the vineyards really gathered momentum, there has been a distinct divergence of opinion among the growers, with the result that there are now two *syndicats* in Chablis, with opposing attitudes towards the growth of the vineyard area.

The original *syndicat* of 1960 is now called Le Syndicat de la Défense de l'Appellation de Chablis. Its members consist mainly of growers in Chablis and the immediately adjacent villages and, as its name implies, it is in favour of the strict delimitation of Chablis. It is headed by William Fèvre, of Domaine de la Maladière, who fervently believes in the importance of the kimmeridgian limestone. He has fought the INAO's decision to expand the vineyard area by lodging an appeal with the Conseil d'Etat, but to no avail: the Conseil d'Etat has upheld the decision of the INAO.

The second and newer *syndicat*, called La Fédération des Viticulteurs Chablisiens, is led by Jean Durup, of Domaine de l'Eglantière, in Maligny. His members consist mainly of those growers in the outlying villages, such as Lignorelles, Villy and Maligny, whose vineyards are those most affected by the decisions of the INAO. Needless to say, as they would benefit from the expansion, they are in favour of enlarging the appellation of Chablis.

As far as the INAO is concerned, the situation is now settled, but for the growers of Chablis there are still doubts. The argument over the extension of the vineyards depends on the famous kimmeridgian limestone. 'Kimmeridge' is the rallying cry of William Fèvre's *syndicat*;

they believe that the original decision of the Tribunal de Tonnerre of 1923 that defined Chablis according to the extent of the kimmeridgian limestone should be upheld. It was unfortunate that kimmeridge was not mentioned in the 1929 judgement, but this omission was remedied by the CNAO in 1938. William Fèvre believes that the INAO is now making a grave error in permitting the extension of the vineyards and that it has compromised the quality of Chablis by allowing vines to be planted in areas that he believes to be completely unsuitable.

Although it cannot be disputed that soil has an effect on the quality and style of a wine, it is only a contributory factor. Microclimate and the winemaker's technical expertise are as important. Bill Jekel, of Jekel Winery in California, has argued[1] that the mineral components of the soil contribute little or nothing to the quality of a wine, but that it is the physical structure of the soil (which determines the environment of the roots) that is vitally important. Like most Californians he believes that the microclimate is of greater significance than the soil in determining the quality of a wine.

As we have seen, the experts examining the terrain after the 1938 decree failed to agree as to whether certain areas should be included within the demarcation of kimmeridgian soil. Perhaps the importance of geological definitions (which, in this context, must be very arbitrary) has been exaggerated. At any rate, the INAO now believes this to be so, as Pierre Bréjoux has explained.[2]

The expansionist *syndicat* believes in the necessity of extending the vineyards for commercial reasons. The average production of two thousand hectares of vines is a very small drop of wine on the world market: it is more desirable, the *syndicat* thinks, that the vineyard area should be extended to include areas that produce acceptable Chablis than to increase the yields of existing vineyards to excess. The Chardonnay is capable of very high yields; in Chablis it has on occasion produced as much as a hundred hectolitres per hectare, or more, but it would not be desirable to make this a regular practice.

The controversy has not been without its moments of drama. One afternoon Chablis would have provided a suitable setting for an episode from *Clochemerle*. A headline in the local newspaper, *Le Yonne Républicain*, for 21 September 1973, read, 'Du Rififi pour le Chablis. Quand l'avion et le talkie walkie entrent dans la bataille de l'appellation.'

[1] 'Factors for Fine Wine', *Decanter*, August 1982.
[2] 'Le Chablis'.

The ensuing article went on to describe an attempt by William Fèvre and his supporters to survey some land in the northern part of the Chablisien. Durup's men decided that they should be stopped, and so Michel Laroche, another expansionist, took off in his private aeroplane, with a walkie talkie connection to the ground, to plot their progress. He said that he had spent a very entertaining afternoon, and on the ground the consumption of Chablis rose dramatically, but not much else was achieved.

The story of the Bois de Milly is another example of the use – or abuse – of the expansionist programme. It concerns a wood above the Côte de Léchet, south-facing and with soil more portlandian than kimmeridgian. The parcel of woodland was bought by a Parisian, Pierre des Courtis, ostensibly to build a house. Instead he obtained permission, no doubt with the help of the expansionist *syndicat*, to cut down the trees and plant a vineyard. It was first designated as Petit Chablis, but was quickly promoted to Chablis, much to the consternation of the restrictionist *syndicat*.

William Fèvre has voiced his opinions in his occasional satirical newspaper *Le Chablis Républicain* ('un journal satirique paraissant de temps à autre le mercredi à Chablis issu de la résistance à la médiocrité'). Constant reference is made to 'les usages locaux, loyaux et constants', upon which the appellation regulations are based. He accuses certain less principled growers of changing the contours of their vineyards by moving the soil with bulldozers and trucks. This theme is also taken up in Pierre Marie Doutrelant's cynical survey of the wines of France.[1] The chapter on Chablis is very caustic and, I believe, presents a ridiculously exaggerated view of the expansion of the vineyards, summed up in the phrase 'when the public authorities judge that the best way of combating fraud is to make its practice legal'.

Demands were made to reclassify the vineyards, including one from a grower 'who had the nerve to insist on the inclusion in Chablis *premier cru* of a corner of land quite unsuitable for any cultivation, but on which he had managed to plant vines after breaking up and levelling the ground with bulldozers and adding twenty thousand cubic metres of alluvial soil from elsewhere. *Premiers crus* for a cabbage patch and a prefabricated vineyard.'

The other side of the story is that the soil of the slopes of Fourchaume had eroded; all that was happening was the time-honoured practice of

---

[1] *Les Bons Vins et les Autres.*

restoring the soil to its rightful position on the hillsides.

As well as his polemical news-sheet, William Fèvre has argued his case in his pamphlet *Le Vrai Chablis et Les Autres*. Apart from discussing the abuse of the name of Chablis elsewhere in the world, he categorically states his opinions as to the present expansion of the vineyards of Chablis. He is insistent that the decisions of the INAO do not take into account 'les usages locaux, loyaux et constants' and that areas have been classified that in no way merit the appellation. In particular, he mentions two hundred hectares of newly classified *premiers crus*, of which only fifteen hectares were already planted with vines. The greater part was woodland and *friche* (wasteland), some areas of which bore rather unfortunate names like Verjus ('sour grapes') and 'Les Champs des Raves' ('turnip fields').

The argument for the classification of the new *premiers crus* is that the land is of similar aspect, with a similar microclimate and terrain, as that of the existing *premiers crus*, and that logically, therefore, the wine which it yields should be of similar quality. In theory, the growers who have invested in these new *premiers crus*, without knowing whether the quality of their wine will justify the investment, will be able, if they say that quality is their *sole* aim, to assess their wine objectively and not sell it as Chablis Premier Cru unless they sincerely feel that its quality justifies the appellation. In practice, there is the danger, and indeed the likelihood, that greed and the need for a return on their investment will override considerations of quality. The new plantings of *premiers crus* came into production with the 1983 vintage and have indeed been judged to be of sufficient quality to merit the classification of Chablis *premier cru*.

Every year the INAO decides how much land can be planted, acting on the advice of the *syndicats* (see Appendix 5). Even if permission to plant is granted, this does not mean that it will always be immediately taken up.

Attitudes vary among the growers. Some are disenchanted by the politics of the situation and consider that both presidents have used their *syndicats* for their own financial aims and political purposes (as indeed they have), and a few of these growers have withdrawn from membership of either *syndicat*. Other growers willingly admit that they have benefited from the expansion and support it, but within reason, for there is the danger that too fast an expansion will adversely affect the quality of Chablis. It is generally accepted that the older vines, of thirty or fifty years' age, produce wines of greater character and depth of flavour, as their root systems are better developed and they are thus able to reach otherwise unobtainable mineral resources. They are also better able to withstand long periods without rain, such as the summer of 1982, when the leaves on the young vines were turning yellow, even before the vintage. At present the average age of the vines in the vineyards of Chablis is fifteen to twenty years, which is an acceptable age, but if the vineyard area were to be extended with plantations of new vines so that the average age of the vines fell to any great extent, the overall quality of Chablis would suffer, irrespective of the terrain and other considerations. A vine takes four years to yield *appellation contrôlée* wine at all and ten years to reach its peak of production. If it has an undeveloped root system it will be unable to give the nuances of flavour characteristic of a wine produced from older vines.

Other growers, like Alain Geoffroy, the Mayor of Beines (which is one of the communes most affected by the expansion), see the growth in the vineyards not as an extension, but as a revision. There were 350 hectares of vines in Beines before the phylloxera crisis; after the Second World War, there were only thirty-five. Geoffroy would like to see the vineyards of Beines restored to their former importance – an aim which he is not far from achieving since, as a result of fresh plantings, there were 280 hectares by 1982. The Société d'Aménagement Foncier d'Etablissement Rural (SAFER), a government organization that controls rural development in France, has helped with the planting of the new vineyards in the commune. However, one grower from Chablis itself muttered that traditionally the worst Chablis has always come from Beines.

The more conservative growers fear that the extension is taking place too fast. One described the growth as 'la folie furieuse'; another spoke of 'la marée montante ('rising tide') de la vigne autour de Chablis'. References were made to 'la banalisation de Chablis' caused by the excessive expansion. There are fears that the reputation of Chablis, as well as its quality, will suffer.

The fault lies partly with the INAO (run by bureaucrats, and subject to multiple political pressures), which has persistently failed to define the vineyards of Chablis: even today the *premiers crus* are not yet completely delimited. The INAO had also left loopholes by its early failure to delimit the vineyards of Petit Chablis, and these anomalies left the way open to speculation and disagreements.

The position of the classification of Petit Chablis is somewhat ambiguous. As I have mentioned (p. 38), the appellation was reinstated in 1944 with the aim of differentiating between the wine grown on kimmeridgian and on portlandian soils in the northern part of the vineyard. Petit Chablis was designated the production of the Chardonnay grape on portlandian soil, whereas Chablis was produced on kimmeridgian soil. Traditionally, it is considered to be a *vin de primeur*, with no potential for ageing. The possibility of renaming the wine has been discussed, and the name Chablis Village has been suggested; but elsewhere in Burgundy – and, indeed, in France as a whole – the addition of the word *village* implies that the wine is better than that which bears the basic name, and so even further confusion would have been caused. As a wine name, Petit Chablis sounds rather deprecating, almost petty, rather than *petit*, and its commercial success seems doubtful. In Britain, before *appellation contrôlée* was accepted at the time of the country's entry into the Common Market in 1973, most Petit Chablis was relabelled Chablis. Today there is a definite decline in the vineyards of Petit Chablis; the better sites, with better aspects, have been upgraded into Chablis – most notably in the area around Maligny, where the Durup *syndicat* is strongest and the lesser vineyards on the plateaus have been eliminated. In 1976 there were 184 hectares of Petit Chablis; by 1981, only 113. Most growers expect that the name will eventually disappear completely.

The growth of the vineyard area has resulted in a great deal of investment and speculation in Chablis, in a few cases by people without any real interest in the wine and the region. On the other hand, many of the large estates which have been created over the last twenty years (and which now operate on an industrial scale) are based on the original family holdings. In fact, there have been very few total newcomers to the area, but the earlier trend of rural depopulation has been reversed, with former natives of the region returning to it to take over their parents' property, now that the incentive is stronger and the rewards of the Chablis vineyard greater. The interest among young people who wish to establish themselves in the area, rather than succumbing to the lure of Paris, is also considerable. Despite the enlargement of some *domaines*, small family holdings still exist.

Jean Durup said in May 1981 that the *syndicats* were 'en repos'. Let us hope so. It is perhaps unwise to dwell too long on the dissensions which I have outlined above. Most growers will tell you that quality is their objective above all. If the expansion or revision of the vineyards is carried out at a moderate, reasonable pace, and the new plantings are made conscientiously, the quality of Chablis should not suffer and the vineyards will be better able to meet the demands of a world market.

3

VITICULTURE: THE FIGHT AGAINST THE FROST

The character of any wine is determined by four basic factors: the grape variety, the soil in which it is grown, the climatic conditions to which it is subject and the human element that decides the way in which the vine is treated and the wine is made. Two of these elements are constant; they are the grape variety and the soil, the combination of which determines the basic character of a wine. The climate, especially in a very northerly vineyard, can vary considerably from year to year and it is these variations that give the wine its annual individuality or personality. Finally, the human element accounts for the nuances of variation to be found in wines which, being produced in a small vineyard belonging to several people, are otherwise of identical origin.

The Chardonnay Grape

Like all fine white Burgundy, Chablis is made from the Chardonnay grape, which in the Yonne was commonly called the Beaunois, possibly because it came to the region from Beaune. Its origins are uncertain. There is a village in the Mâconnais called Chardonnay, whose name, however, may well have originated from the cultivation of Chardonnay in the region. According to P. Galet,[1] the Chardonnay was for a long time believed to be the white version of the Pinot Noir, but this has now been disproved, and, despite current confusion with the use of the term Pinot Chardonnay, there is no relationship between the two vines.

Chardonnay is a vigorous grape variety, with a good resistance to low winter temperatures. Its early bud break makes it susceptible to the spring frosts that so often occur in Chablis, but this is compensated for by its early maturity, which enables it to be grown in areas with a short growing season. Its yield can vary quite considerably, depending on the richness of the soil and climatic conditions, ranging from fifteen hectolitres per hectare, or less, to a hundred or more. Although it has some resistance to downy mildew, Chardonnay is sensitive to powdery mildew and to *botrytis*.

[1] *Cépages et Vignobles de France.*

47

P. Galet gives a list of synonyms for Chardonnay: Chardennet, Chardenai, Chardonnet, Chaudenay, Pinot Blanc (Cramant), Pinot blanc Chardonnay (Marne), Arnaison blanc, Arnoison (Touraine), Aubaine, Auvernat blanc, Auxois blanc, Auxerrois blanc (Lorraine), Beaunois (Chablis), Epinette blanche (Champagne), Morillon blanc (Yonne), Arvoisier (Aube), Blanc de Cramant (Marne), Rousseau or Roussot (Val de Saône), Gamay blanc (Lons-le-Saunier), Moulon (Poligny), Melon blanc (Arbois), Luisant (Besancon), Noirien blanc and Chaudenet (Côte Chalonnaise), Plant de Tonnerre (Yonne), Mâconnais (Isère), Petite Saint-Marie (Savoie), Petit Chatey (Jura), Weisser Clevner or Klawner (Germany, Alsace).

Soil

As has been discussed in Chapter 2, the soil of Chablis is a subject of dispute and controversy in relation to the expansion of the vineyards. However, from the point of view of viticulture, suffice it to say that the soil is *argilo-calcaire* (calcareous clay), be it kimmeridgian, portlandian or some other kind. The vineyards lie close to the rim of the Paris basin, where the rocks date back to the Upper Jurassic age, some 180 million years ago, which makes the basin older than the Alps. On the other edge of the basin is the Dorset village of Kimmeridge, which gives its name to this geological formation and period. There is clay, which is badly drained, but there are also lime-rich muds, packed with fossil shells of a small oyster, *exogyra virgula*, so that the vineyards of Chablis are, appropriately, situated on what is virtually an oyster fossil bank. The abundance of shells gives the soil a very high percentage of lime, as much as fifty per cent, so that the soil is pale-grey, almost white in colour. Because of its high lime content the soil is very porous, with excellent drainage, so that the problem of erosion of soil on the vineyard slopes does not usually arise.

Chappaz and Rousseau, who were the first commentators to mention the importance of kimmeridgian soil for Chablis, have also analysed the other soil constituents of the Chablis vineyards.[1] They found the level of nitrate to be low, that of magnesium satisfactory, that of potassium high and that of phosphorous also well above average. All the soil ingredients which are necessary for the production of healthy vines and excellent wines are, therefore, present.

[1] *Etude sur le Vignoble de Chablis.*

The gentle Serein flows through the centre of Chablis

The slopes of the vineyards of Chablis, with the town in the distance

The two methods of frost protection: aspersion (left) and *chaufferettes* burning (right)
Young vine buds covered in a protective coat of ice; this is how the aspersion method of frost protection protects the vine

Climate

The combination of the Chardonnay vine with clay and limestone soil accounts for the basic character of Chablis. A third element is provided by the climate, which is essentially semi-continental, without maritime influence. The winters are long and hard, and the summers fairly hot.

TEMPERATURE AND SUNSHINE

Professor Amerine[1] stresses the importance of temperature during the growing season. The period of growth for a vine begins in the early spring (when the average temperature reaches 10°C, and the débourrement, or bud-break, occurs with the general warming up of the atmosphere) and finishes with the fall of leaves in the autumn. The time between these two stages varies between 259 days in Montpellier and 180 days in Chablis and Reims. Effective temperature is measured in 'degree days'. The average daily temperatures, above 10°C, are taken and added together during the growing period, from 1 April to 31 October, to give a total, in the case of Chablis of 1087°C. This is very close to the coldest limit. As the table in Appendix 9 shows, Champagne (Reims) is the only French wine region which is colder than Chablis.

At Chablis, far away from the influence of the sea and its moderating effects, there are wide variations of temperature from year to year. It is hard to talk of a typical Chablis year, and there is certainly no direct relationship between final harvest quality and a particular theoretical optimum range of degree day value. The vintage of 1971 had 1135°C, the larger and less good vintage of 1973 had more degree days at 1271°C, and 1972, the worst vintage of the decade, had 800°C.

Hours of sunshine are also significant, as is the ambient temperature, for the vine needs sunshine in order to photosynthesize and allow the leaves to assimilate the sugar that will eventually produce ripe grapes. Taking the amounts of sunshine from the relevant months of April to September, Chablis has an average of 1,285 hours, compared to Dijon (1,433 hours), Reims (1,190 hours) and Montpellier (1,771 hours). The differences between Chablis, Dijon and Reims are not very great, but, with over 500 more hours of sunshine in Montpellier, it is easy to see the advantages enjoyed by the Midi in the production of ripe grapes.

---

[1] *The Technology of Winemaking.*

FROST

Frost is the over-riding preoccupation in early spring, because it is expected that the yield will be affected. The narrow valley of the Serein is particularly susceptible to frost, which settles on the lower slopes and attacks the *grands crus* vineyards in particular. All the vineyards, however, are vulnerable to frost damage from the end of March until the middle of May. Nevertheless, an examination of the eighteen years 1963–80 suggests some surprising conclusions. The plethoric year of 1979 saw a great deal of frost. On the other hand, during the three great vintage years of the 1970s (1971, 1975 and 1978) there was almost no frost in May, and perhaps the buds were therefore in better condition, with the result that they produced better grapes later. Finally, the disastrous year of 1972 was almost frost-free in the spring, but, very unusually, had frost in September. The conclusion, perhaps, is that frost is a negligible factor, as long as the grower protects his vines against it (a subject to which I shall return later).

RAINFALL AND HAIL

Rainfall has a direct effect on the amount of juice there is in the grapes, on the sugar levels and on the concentration of grape must. There are no particularly wet or dry months. In winter there is a great deal of light rain, whereas in summer there are fewer days of rain, but it is heavier, with storms. The recipe for a great vintage is clear: no rain in September and up to the vintage, as in 1971, 1975 and 1978. The effect of rainfall on quantity was only too apparent in 1979, when rainfall in August, September and October was well above average.

Number of days of 1 cm rainfall or more

	July	*August*	*September*	*October*
1971	2	5	0	0
1975	2	2	1	0
1978	1	0	0	1
1979	1	4	2	5

The October data cannot be interpreted directly, because it is not known whether the rain fell before, during or after the vintage.

Hail is another hazard, which can cause considerable localized damage. May is the month of greatest risk, with a statistical possibility of three days of hail. From February to April the risk is two days; in the other months of the year, one day. However (as is not the case with frost), insurance against hail is possible, although expensive.

MICROCLIMATE

In an area so near the cold extremity of practical grape-growing, questions of microclimate and the exposure to the sun of individual hillsides are of critical importance. Chablis, at the junction of the south-north river valley and east and west lesser valleys, has an immeasurable advantage in microclimate compared to other sites in the Yonne. The best vineyards of Chablis, those that receive the most sunshine, are situated on the right bank of the Serein, with south-west-facing slopes.

The *grands crus* have the steepest and longest slopes, broken by small valleys. The vineyards of the *premiers crus* on the left bank of the Serein face south-east and therefore have slightly less sunshine than those on the right bank. The angle of the vineyard slope is also significant, for it is on this that the concentration of sunshine depends. If the vineyards face south, a 20° to 30° slope is best. If, however, the vineyards are north-facing, as are some Chablis and Petit Chablis vineyards, the slope needs to be more gentle, in order to obtain the maximum benefit from the sun's rays.

Apart from the valley of the Serein, there are other tiny valleys, each of which creates its own particular microclimate, so that vineyards may be protected from the wind, but more or less exposed to the sun and rain. A small part of the vineyards of Valmur and Grenouilles does in fact face north, but their microclimate is such that the quality of their wine is unaffected.

The other constant factor in the vineyards is their altitude. The vineyards of Chablis are situated between 130 and 270 metres above sea level. Nevertheless, temperatures can vary quite considerably within this range, especially as far as frost is concerned.

The GETEVAY

Before discussing the work of the *viticulteur* in the Chablisien, it is necessary first to mention the Groupement d'Etude Technique Viticole et Arboricole de l'Yonne (GETEVAY), an organization which plays an important role in the viticultural life of the area. It was founded in 1957 by a group of *viticulteurs* in an attempt to save (if that is not too drastic a word to use) the vineyards of Chablis by developing a system of frost protection. The responsibilities of the GETEVAY have, however, since become greatly enlarged, and they now cover all the viticultural and oenological problems that the growers are likely to encounter. Nearly all the growers of the Yonne belong to the organization, which now has at its disposal two technical experts: an agricultural engineer (who is also responsible for the cherry-trees in the region, as well as viticultural problems) and an oenological adviser. The GETEVAY conducts experiments in new products and methods, helps with the construction of cellars and gives advice where it is needed on a particular problem. It has a laboratory for analysis. In 1981, 3,700 samples of wine were tested, either to solve a specific problem or to determine the evolution of a wine. Regular bulletins are issued, giving details of new developments and treatments, and visits to other French and foreign vineyards are organized – all in the cause of furthering the members' knowledge. Altogether, the GETEVAY plays a very valuable role by assisting the growers in the development of the wines of the area and in maintaining their quality.

The Advent of the Tractor

There have been two dramatic developments in the vineyards of Chablis over the past thirty years: the advent of the tractor and the invention of effective frost protection techniques.

Mechanization has revolutionized the character of the vineyards; the *viticulteur*'s work has been transformed, as have the size and use of his land. Chablis was slow to accept mechanization. Robert Vocoret was the first grower to have a tractor (in 1951), but his example was not followed by others until about 1957. Previously a grower and his wife could only expect to cultivate two or three hectares of vines, without any extra help, whereas today an average of six or seven hectares is possible. Before the tractor came into use, a grower needed two horses and the land to support them: a couple of hectares of lucerne, about three hectares of oats and a hectare or two of barley. In addition to their horses, most growers also had a couple of cows, and not only did they have grapes to pick, but there was also hay-making in June. There were even cherry- and walnut-trees in the middle of some vineyards. Before the development of reliable frost protection methods, the climatic uncertainties of the region made it impossible for a grower to rely solely on his vines for his livelihood; polyculture was the norm. Once tractors were accepted, however, the growers sold their horses and cows and, with the incentive of the more reliable yields which resulted from effective frost protection, planted their agricultural land with vines.

Tractors have not only contributed to the growth of the vineyards, but have also helped to improve their hygiene. Working in the vineyards is much less arduous than it used to be. Guy Moreau remembers beginning work in the vines with the sunrise. They sprayed the vines with the traditional sulphur mixture, the *bouille bordelaise*, which was carried on the back. Now the spraying can be done from a tractor. Some growers even use a helicopter, but only a few, except for those whose vineyards have very steep slopes, since helicopters are not considered to be particularly efficient, especially when there is a strong wind and it is not possible to fly low enough and close enough to the vines. But even with a tractor, the *viticulteur*'s task in Chablis is not an easy one.

Mechanization was to be taken a stage further in the 1970s, when mechanical harvesters were used in the Yonne for the first time, as I shall describe in due course.

Frost Protection Methods

Important as the coming of mechanization was, it was the introduction of effective frost protection methods which revolutionized the financial viability of the vineyards of Chablis. The decade of the 1950s demonstrates the hardship caused by inclement weather: there were only four years of normal production, compared to three years of almost complete devastation by frost and three years with only half a crop. It was at the end of this decade that the first tentative attempts at frost protection were made.

Guy Moreau remembers burning little pots of fuel in the vineyards in the spring of 1957. It was very hard work, as everything was done by hand. The *viticulteur* had to be in the vineyard to light each pot, usually at three o'clock in the morning, and each pot then had to be refilled the following morning. However, from these primitive beginnings there have developed the two principal methods of frost protection used in the Chablis vineyards: the aspersion method, and the use of heaters of various kinds. Neither technique is perfect; each has its advantages and disadvantages. Aspersion – the spraying of the vines to form a protective coating of ice – works on the principle that water freezes at 0°C, and that a vine will not suffer damage from frost until the temperature falls to about −5°C. The photographs taken by Alain Geoffroy during the severe frosts of 1981 demonstrate this perfectly, showing the young buds in a snug coating of ice (facing p. 49). For the protection to be effective, the spraying must start as soon as the temperature reaches zero and it must continue for as long as the temperature remains at or below freezing-point. If there is ever any interruption in the water spray, the damage to the vines will be even more severe than if no precautions had been taken in the first place. It sounds foolproof but it is, in fact, fraught with hazards. When the sprinklers are blocked, which can easily happen, this may not be immediately apparent in the poor visibility of the early hours of the morning. In 1981 one grower lost eighteen hectares of vines when a vital pipe burst and his entire system of frost protection collapsed.

The effectiveness of the aspersion method depends on there being little or no wind; otherwise the spray will be blown off the vines, and even on to a neighbour's vines. Again, in 1981 there were problems when the spring frosts, which normally settle on the valley floor, were blown up the vineyard slopes. Another disadvantage is that the melting ice makes the vineyards very muddy. However, the success of aspersion has been such that by 1980 over two hundred hectares of the Chablisien were protected in this way. A large reservoir was built by a group of some thirty growers outside Beines to service an aspersion system for eighty hectares of vines, principally of Fourchaume. It has been in operation since 1978 and now works well, after some initial teething troubles caused by tiny fish getting into the system and blocking the pumps!

The installation costs for an aspersion system are high and, once installed, the equipment has to be maintained, but these expenses are offset by minimal labour costs.

Various methods of heating the vineyards have been tried, ranging from traditional paraffin *chaufferettes* to infra-red devices and automatic fuel heaters. The traditional, manually-filled chaufferettes are now being abandoned and automatic fuel heating systems are being installed, with burners connected to a nearby fuel tank. The burners are filled under pressure, once the equipment has been set in motion. Many people feel that this is a much more efficient and reliable system. The

Installation of automatically controlled heating in one of the *grand cru* Chablis vineyards. The town of Chablis can be seen in the background

main problem is the cost of the fuel: sixty thousand francs for six nights over seven hectares of *grands crus* vineyards in 1981, which, taking an average yield of thirty-one hectolitres per hectare in the *grands crus*, would add over two francs to the cost of each bottle of wine. Perhaps that is a very small price to pay to ensure that the wine will be produced at all. However, the labour costs are also much higher than with aspersion systems, as the burners have to be lit individually; this necessitates a couple of men per hectare.

The control of frost has also been helped by the expansion of the vineyard area, as many of the growers have consolidated their holdings and there are now far fewer parcels of uncultivated land in the midst of the vines; with more condensed areas of vines, there is less risk of frost. The increased use of weed killers has also lessened the risk of frost damage. With fewer weeds, there is less humidity in the air and therefore less danger of frost. The use of weed-killers also takes away the need to disturb the soil of the vineyards and thereby reduces the amount of humidity given off by the soil.

The Station Météorologique at St Georges d'Auxerre plays an important role in helping the growers to fight the frost. Depending on the state of the vegetation of the vines, but usually from the end of March until well into May, a warning system is in operation. The station is able to calculate the likelihood of frost by using the Brunt formula which, it was explained to me, takes into account the temperature at four o'clock in the afternoon, the level of humidity and the length of the night. They can calculate the fall in temperature during the night, allowing for a correction to be made for wind and cloud cover. Altitude also affects the temperature, to the extent that there may be a difference of 2° to 2.5°C between the top and bottom of a vineyard slope. The formula works best with a clear sky and no wind, for the effects of cloud cover and wind are difficult to predict. Like any weather forecast, it is a 'guestimate', but the station has rarely made a serious mistake. It issues three bulletins a day, as a recorded telephone message, intended especially for the growers of Chablis.

Viticultural Methods

The treatment of the vines and the work in the vineyards does not differ greatly from practice in other parts of France. The vines in the Chablisien are planted in rows 1.60 to 1.80 metres apart, with a space of one metre between each vine, giving a density of 5,500 to 6,200 plants per hectare. The direction of the rows follows the natural slope of the hillsides.

The nature of the soil determines the choice of rootstock; in Chablis, with the high content of lime and consequently a high risk of chlorosis, it is essential to have a graft that is chlorosis and lime resistant. The two more common grafts therefore are the 41B and, more recently, the berlandieri-based SO4, which is not only successful on limestone, but also gives grapes with a higher sugar content, particularly in difficult years, and ripens earlier – as much as fourteen days earlier than the 41B. Experiments are also being carried out with a new graft, Fercal, which is only about six or seven years old; it is even more resistant to chlorosis than 41B and has an earlier maturity. The 3309 and 161–49 have now virtually disappeared from the Chablisien.

Tradition has it that the donkey taught man to prune his vines, when it was observed that vines that had suffered from a passing donkey's voracious appetite grew more prolifically the following year than their neighbours, which had not suffered in the same way. The pruning system of Chablis is the double *guyot*, with two fruit-bearing canes bent in the same direction, usually downhill. The vines are usually supported by three wires, at 60, 75 and 90 cm from the ground. As soon as the risk of frost is over, the canes will be attached to the lower wires so that the grapes will benefit from the radiation of heat absorbed from the ground. This operation is called *baissage* and usually takes place in the second half of May. By the end of May the vines are in full growth, bearing witness to an old Chablis saying: 'A Pentecôte on voit la vigne, de côte à côte.' It is true that at the beginning of May the slopes on either side of the valley are still bare, but by Whitsun they have turned green. (The *taille Chablis* that is used today in Champagne is the pruning system that was used in Chablis during the nineteenth century.)

Work in the vineyards continues throughout the summer. Treatments for *oidium*, mildew and red spider are carried out six times a year, with the appropriate copper- and sulphur-based sprays. *Oidium* has recently reappeared in the Chablisien, as there has, over recent years, been a certain complacency among the growers, who have neglected to treat the vines with sulphur to an adequate extent.

The combination of heat and humidity in the summer makes the vines susceptible to rot, or *pourriture grise*. The first chemical treatments for rot (in the early 1970s) were not very successful, but since the late seventies considerable advances have been made. Three treatments are usually necessary: *à la fleur*, *à la nouaison* (after the fertilization of the grape) and a month before the vintage. Some are of the opinion that these sprays slow down the ripening process; others say that this is a visual deception. There is certainly a danger of spraying too close in time to the vintage, thereby entailing the risk of difficulty in starting the fermentation. However, despite the new sprays, there were problems with rot in 1981, the reasons for which no one has been able to establish with certainty. The GETEVAY is working on a study of the vegetation and climatic elements of the region in order to decide on the right moment to treat against rot, so that just one treatment will be necessary, rather than the recommended three or four. Some growers, such as Adhémar Boudin, have reservations about the anti-*pourriture* sprays. In the first year when they were available (1978) Boudin did not use them and consequently had a quantity of rotten grapes on his hands. And so, after good results were obtained in 1979 by fellow-growers who did use the sprays, in 1980 he resorted to them for the first time, with success. However, in 1981, although he continued with the sprays, he experienced problems with rot once more and felt rather *déçu*. Nevertheless, he decided to carry on with the treatment in 1982.

THE DATE OF THE VINTAGE

The date of the vintage ('le ban de vendange') is announced by prefectoral decree, on the advice of the growers' *syndicats*, after consideration of the particular conditions of the year and in conjunction with the INAO. This is a revival (since 1979) of a traditional custom which had been discontinued at the beginning of the century. Albert Pic refers to the 'ban de vendange' as the day chosen for the beginning of the vintage by the most experienced *vignerons*. 'Cette mesure, survivance des anciens régimes, empêchait les impatients de vendanger trop tôt des raisins incomplètement mûrs; c'était une sage mesure de prévoyance, dont il faut peut-être regretter l'abolition.' ('This measure, surviving from the old regime, prevented impatient growers from harvesting too early grapes that were still unripe; it was a wise preventative measure the abolition of which is to be regretted.')

In his cellars at Coulanges-la-Vineuse, Serge Hugot has an old chart, that he retrieved from somebody's dustbin, giving the dates of the 'bans de vendange' in the Yonne from 1700 to 1893, the year that phylloxera seriously affected the Yonne. The dates are listed, for their historical interest, in Appendix 1. The earliest recorded date was 5 September (in 1822); the latest, 30 October (in 1815). But ignoring these extremes, the vintage for nearly two centuries usually occurred at some time between 22 September and 15 October, the mean date being 3 October, and almost two-thirds of the dates fall in the two weeks between 27 September and 11 October. Perhaps the fact that 1 October occurs more frequently than any other date is accounted for by the tidy mind of the Prefect. This very wide time-span reflects the inconstant climate of Chablis; nor is there any significant difference to indicate any climatic changes between the two centuries.

MECHANICAL HARVESTING

Today the biggest preoccupation in the vineyard is that of mechanical harvesting, according to M. Estançon of the GETEVAY. Mechanical harvesters are coming to Chablis and the Yonne in increasing numbers, as growers experiment with the machines. Labour costs have risen enormously and the difficulty of predicting the exact date of the vintage and the cost not only of paying, but also of feeding and lodging, the *vendangeurs* has forced several growers to consider this alternative.

The first experiments took place between 1974 and 1978, mainly with a machine that is no longer in production. Other machines have been tried out since. In 1981 there were three different types of machine in use, mainly in the Auxerrois, rather than in Chablis itself. Jean Brocard, who has vineyards in both areas, was the first grower to use a machine in the Chablisien, and in 1982 about ten machines were used in the Yonne, including Chablis.

The INAO has set up a technical commission to study the question, but the general opinion is that, whatever they decide, they will be presented with a *fait accompli*, although the INAO insists that it is reserving the right to reject or accept the machines. Initially their attitude was very lax, as was demonstrated by their *laissez-faire* policy in Bordeaux. It is also worth noting that in Champagne and Beaujolais mechanical harvesters cannot be used, as the appellation regulations insist on the picking of whole grapes. The majority of the machines currently in production are too wide for use in the Chablis vineyards, for which smaller and narrower models are needed.

The GETEVAY has been closely following the results obtained with mechanical harvesters. The first obvious difference is in the *taux d'éclatement*. In a vintage gathered by traditional methods virtually all the grapes are whole, whereas, when a mechanical harvester has been used, only about thirty to forty per cent of the grapes are intact. Negligible differences in the quality of the fermentation have been observed. In taste, a very slight difference is apparent, in that a young wine (a year old) seems more perfumed, as it has undergone an aeration (an oxygenation as opposed to an oxidation), which accelerates the ageing process slightly. In fact, the changes are likely to be more obvious in the red wines of the Yonne, which are not usually destalked before fermentation, since, with mechanical harvesters, the grapes are automatically destalked.

There is also the question of the speed of the vintage. If the machine is operated carefully and slowly, there will be no problems, but if it is operated fast, on a group basis or in order to obtain an hourly amount, a reduction in the quality of the grapes will occur. There is perhaps something to be said for conscientious grape-pickers.

Another consideration is the suitability of the vineyards. In the best vineyards of the *grands crus* the slopes are too steep for the use of the machines at all. In vineyards where they can be used, the wires have to be raised slightly and all the canes have to be systematically trained the same way. However, the principle normally followed is to adapt the machines to the vines, rather than vice versa, as was done in the Midi.

A possible side effect of the use of mechanical harvesters is the presence of rust in the juice and thereby of iron in the wine. Consequently, experiments are being conducted with galvanized iron and stainless-steel wires. Plastic has been found to be unsatisfactory.

CLONAL SELECTION

The other significant recent innovation in the vineyards of Chablis is clonal selection. The GETEVAY is researching the subject. They use an experimental vineyard at Beines that belongs to the Chambre d'Agriculture at Auxerre, where about twenty different Chardonnay clones have been planted as well as three of Aligoté. Their work is co-ordinated by the Groupement Régional d'Amélioration et de la Prémultiplication de la Vigne du Centre Est (GRAPVI). So far, six Chardonnay clones have been accepted and a further twenty-five are being closely studied. The clones are tested for their colour, maturity, alcohol, acidity and yield. It is quality rather than quantity that is significant, although yields will increase at the same time as the vines will become healthier and virus-free.

The selection of virus-free vines is vital in dealing with *court noué*, which does exist in the Chablisien. *Court noué* is a virus that is transmitted by nematodes in the soil, through the roots of the vine. Originally, the virus was eliminated naturally when the land was left fallow for as long as twenty years before replanting, for then there was nothing on which the virus could feed and it therefore died. However, with the exigencies of today's economy this is completely impractical. Before replanting today, the soil is disinfected, but this is often ineffective, as the disinfectant does not go deep enough, and the land is left fallow for only a year. Ideally, a combination of the two actions should take place: a disinfection after three years of the land lying fallow, and a further year's wait before replanting. With clonally selected vines, the virus would be destroyed.

Among the growers there are mixed feelings about clonal selection. For Adhémar Boudin 'c'est un merveil' ('it's a marvel'); for William Fèvre, 'le meilleur et le pire' ('the best and the worst'). Many growers feel an underlying concern that clonal selection will bring about a uniformity in the character of the vines, that they will react in exactly the same way (for instance, by flowering at exactly the same time, in perhaps the same bad weather), so that a mixture of clones in a vineyard would be necessary. Others fear an excessive increase in yields. However, I suspect that their reservations are merely the typical conservative reaction to a new-fangled idea. In any case, clonal selection is here to stay, for, from after the beginning of 1984, any plantings must be carried out with clonally-selected vines.

Yields

The final question to consider is that of the yields, for the whole purpose of growing vines is to produce grapes. It is the yield as well as the quality of the grapes that determines the success of each vintage. The commercial significance of the yield is discussed in Chapter 6. What we are concerned with here is the viticultural aspect of the yield.

In the right conditions the Chardonnay is a very prolific grape variety, with a potential yield of a hundred hectolitres per hectare at the moment of budding. This will subsequently be affected by climatic conditions, for even though the vines are treated in an identical way each year, the yield can vary from as little as twenty-seven hectolitres per hectare (1981) to seventy-seven hectolitres (1979). The difference came from the climate. Ten years ago the 1981 vintage would have been completely devastated by frost, and, despite enormous improvements in frost protection, considerable damage was still done. The size of the 1978 vintage was determined by bad weather during flowering. In 1979 there was neither frost nor hail and more than ample rain, and a large vintage was the result.

The vineyards are healthier than they were thirty and even twenty years ago. Before 1950 twenty hectolitres per hectare was the average yield; during the 1950s, twenty-five hectolitres was the norm; in the 1960s, thirty hectolitres; in the 1970s, forty to forty-five hectolitres. This amounts to an increase of 100 per cent in the space of twenty-odd years. Yet within the 1970s there were enormous fluctuations, as Appendix 3 shows. The total crop of the vineyard has also increased enormously, with the expansion of the area during the 1970s.

The pruning of the vine entails a decision concerning the yield on the part of the grower. Much depends on his conscience. Normally, there should be about seven buds per cane, and therefore a total of fourteen per vine, although it can happen that fewer buds will produce more grapes. Pruning also depends on the vigour of the vine, whether it is young or old, and on the terrain in which it is grown. There are no precise appellation regulations about pruning; it is more a question of 'L'Homme propose; la Nature dispose', and human nature dictates that man will propose a large quantity in the anticipation of nature disposing of a high proportion of the potential yield.

As the Chardonnay is a prolific grape variety in the right conditions, there is no reason why a good yield cannot be compatible with high quality. The conditions of the individual vintage are vital: whether the grapes are healthy and free from rot, and whether there has been enough sunshine for them to ripen properly. For instance, in 1979 the average yield was nearly eighty hectolitres per hectare, without any adverse effect on quality, whereas a yield of that size would have been unacceptable in the cooler summer of 1980. In general, however, a much higher yield would throw doubts on the credibility of the vintage.

The annual yield is now determined by the INAO, in conjunction with the growers' *syndicats*. The conditions and quality of the individual year are taken into account, and not unnaturally everyone hopes for as big a yield as possible without, of course, detracting from the quality of the vintage.

4

VINIFICATION: OAK VERSUS STEEL

The making of white wine has improved enormously over the last two decades all over France, and in Chablis as much as anywhere. Everywhere there is a greater understanding of the processes of fermentation and vinification, and there is a greater control of the results. As Bernard Barat, a grower in Milly, said, 'On faisait du vin comme papa autrefois sans trop chercher à comprendre.' Today the dangers of oxidation are appreciated, as well as the occurrence of the malolactic fermentation. Also, improvements in equipment and technical methods have benefited the quality of Chablis.

But fortunately these improvements have not brought about a uniformity in the character of Chablis, since the growers differ so much in method and outlook. For although they all begin with the same basic raw materials, and the final product is always unmistakably Chablis, there is a rich variety of nuance in style and personality between the wines of the various growers – the direct result of their contrasting methods, processes and theories.

The differences begin from the moment the grapes are picked. They are never destalked and the bunches are pressed whole, except on the rare occasions when mechanical harvesters have been used. Most growers use the modern cylindrical presses – either the bright-yellow Vaslin hydraulic presses with two discs, or the gentler bladder presses – which are able to release the juice in the grapes without crushing the tannins in the skins and pips. The must is then allowed to fall clear, a procedure called *débourbage*. Most growers let this happen naturally: Laroche use a centrifuge; Adhémar Boudin fines his must with bentonite. Boudin has discovered that, if this is done, no further fining is necessary once the wine is made – just a light filtration before bottling. However, it is essential that the must is not left too long before fermentation begins, otherwise it will start to oxidize, turning reddish-brown, like an apple. Although this colour change is reversed once the fermentation begins, the ultimate taste of the wine can be affected. A minimum amount of sulphur should be used during the fermentation; Laroche use none at all, as they believe that the malolactic fermentation (a phenomenon which I shall discuss shortly) is adversely affected thereby.

An old press in the cellars of Jean Durup at Maligny

Fermentation

Improved techniques have brought about a greater control of the fermentation process. Most growers ferment their wine either in stainless steel vats, or in cement vats lined with enamel paint or fibre glass, so that the fermentation can be carefully controlled. However there are still a few traditionally minded growers who ferment in wood, both in *foudres* and in *fûts*. *Foudres* of eighteen hectolitres or even larger capacity are to be found in the cellars of Robert Vocoret, Jean Collet and Raoul Gautherin. Guy Robin and Julien Baillard both still sometimes ferment in 225-litre *fûts*, but this decision, I suspect, depends less on preconceived theory than on the size of the vintage and the vat space available.

The disadvantages of fermenting in wood are enormous. It is a very inconvenient process that entails infinitely more work in cleaning and maintaining the barrels than does the use of modern vats. Also, temperature control is much less certain: the temperature of the cellar and of the vats can easily be reduced, but it is much harder to lower the temperature of fermenting must inside a barrel. However, a grower like Robert Vocoret feels that it is worth the trouble, believing that fermentation in wood contributes to the quality of his wines, especially the *grands crus*. William Fèvre, who buys some new *fûts* every year, first mellows the new oak by using them to ferment some of his *grands crus*; in subsequent years, he ages wine in them.

The average fermentation in the Chablisien occurs at a temperature of 18–20°C, reaching a maximum of 25°C. If stainless steel vats are used, the temperature is controlled by *ruissellement*: cold water flowing over the steel, to cool it down. If the vats are of concrete, the control of the temperature is more difficult, and many growers are content to let nature take its course. Some, like Louis Michel, believe that the alcoholic fermentation should be as fast as possible. Others, like Michel Laroche, believe that a much slower fermentation is preferable, lasting for about a month, but with 90 per cent of the fermentation occurring in the first week. The temperature during the first forty-eight hours is about 20°C. This is the moment when there is the risk of too hot a fermentation. The rest of the process is much slower, as the yeasts diminish and die in the increasingly alcoholic environment. Some growers use natural yeast; others prefer cultured yeast, which they obtain either from the oenology faculty of the University of Montpellier or from the Institut Pasteur in Paris.

The most significant discovery of the twentieth century to affect the quality of Chablis is the phenomenon of the malolactic fermentation, by which the malic acid is converted into lactic acid. Until about twenty years ago the growers were completely unaware of this secondary fermentation (which is still not fully understood) and their wine was often bottled before it had occurred. The result was rather green, hard Chablis, with as much acidity as seven grammes per litre. The control of the malolactic fermentation has undoubtedly improved beyond measure the basic quality of Chablis by reducing the natural acidity in the wine. The only way of influencing its occurrence is by heating the cellars, which many growers do. Ideally the malolactic fermentation should occur in the autumn, immediately after the alcoholic fermention, but sometimes it may not take place until the temperature has risen again the following spring. In 1979 François Raveneau noted that the malolactic fermentation of his wine was finished by December, whereas, in May 1981, William Fèvre still had vats of 1980 wine which had not yet finished their *malo*. The malolactic fermentation of the 1980 vintage was slower and longer than usual – a characteristic of the vintage resulting from a higher initial acidity in the wines.

CHAPTALIZATION

Chaptalization (the addition of sugar to the must) is a crucial factor in the making of Chablis, its purpose being to raise the alcohol level and thereby achieve a better balance in the wine. As the vineyards are so close to the geographical and climatic limits of successful wine production, chaptalization is permitted without any special annual authorization by the INAO – which, however, recognizes that it must not be abused and has laid down regulations accordingly. Ideally, Chablis should contain about 12° or 12.5° alcohol, with about 4.5–5 grammes of acidity per litre. This is considered to be the ideal ratio for a balanced wine. Over-chaptalization will completely unbalance the wine, making it too full and rich: Chablis is not meant to resemble Meursault. Also, if it is too high in alcohol, Chablis will tend to age badly, so that it loses all its fruit and only the alcohol will remain. Generally, chaptalization is considered 'un mal nécessaire'. The INAO has decreed that 3.4 kilograms of sugar per hectolitre, and a maximum of 200 kilograms per hectare, are allowed. The implication is that the procedure is rather difficult to control. After all, who is to stop you buying sugar, if you happen to like over-sweet *café au lait*? Most growers in the Chablisien buy their sugar from the nearest sugar beet refinery, at Brienon-sur-Armançon; it is referred to by local cynics as 'le soleil de Brienon'. Ultimately, resort to chaptalization depends on the individual grower's judgement and conscience. Certainly no one should have chaptalized in 1976 and very few found it necessary in 1978, whereas in 1980 it was widely practised to maximum levels – and with good reason, for it undoubtedly helps in mediocre years, when there has not been enough sunshine and the natural alcohol level is too low.

Refrigeration

Another significant treatment that may or may not be carried out is that of refrigeration, to prevent a precipitation of tartrate crystals in bottle. This is an innovation of the last ten years which is now practised by all the *négociants* and increasingly by the growers. The wine is subjected to a temperature of $-4°$ to $-5°C$, depending on the alcoholic content, for eight days, and the resulting tartrate crystals are then filtered out of the wine. The growers who age their wine in wood find that in most years the tartrates precipitate naturally during the cold winter months (although perhaps not so uniformly as would be the case if they used refrigeration), and so they do not have to consider resorting to this treatment. In any case, some growers prefer to let this precipitation occur naturally because they feel that the wine is stunned by the cold treatment, which can make it age prematurely. As Luc Michaut said, 'Je n'ai pas besoin de massacrer mon vin' ('I don't need to massacre my wine'). Really it is the growers who bottle their wine within a year of the vintage who need refrigeration equipment, since they cannot wait for the tartrates to precipitate naturally during the winter months.

Ageing

The greatest element of variation in the style of a grower's Chablis comes from the ageing of his wine: whether to age or not to age; whether to age in vat or in wood; if wood is used, whether the wood should be new or old; whether to bottle early and age in bottle. The arguments for and against the use of wood for ageing Chablis are involved, and the discussion has continued ever since the development of storage materials other than wood. Between the two extremes of opinion lie many variations of view.

Although cement vats lined with glass first appeared at the beginning of this century, these were not found outside the cellars of the more sophisticated *négociants*. The small growers continued unquestioningly to use the traditional oak *feuillettes* of 132 litres until the 1950s. When wine was sold in bulk, as it generally was, it was sold with the *feuillette*, and up to the First World War many of the growers were also *tonneliers*, or coopers, who could make their own *feuillettes*. The craft of the *tonnelier*, however, which still flourished in those days, is now sadly dying out. The size of the traditional Chablis barrel (132 litres) is much smaller than that of the *pièce* (228 litres) of the Côte d'Or. This difference in size is accounted for by the poverty of the soil of the Chablisien and the small, stunted oak-trees that grew in the Yonne as a consequence. And so, at a time when local oak would have been used, the *feuillette* was the largest type of barrel that could feasibly be made. But today no oaks are grown in the region at all. As a result, the local growers either buy their barrels from the Côte d'Or or use oak from the Allier or Saône et Loire. Today, the larger *pièces* are more common than the traditional *feuillette*.

It is indisputable that the prevention of oxidation, or excessive oxidation, is essential in the making of white wine, to which oxygen is basically harmful. What is open to question is the extent to which the ageing of Chablis in wood contributes to the character of the wine, or detracts from its quality. The modern school of thought abhors the use of oak, believing that the demand today is for a young, fresh style of wine, and that the use of wood can no longer contribute anything to it. An oak flavour, however subtle, is not an element of quality in a wine, and it is argued by some that oak is not a suitable medium for a wine like Chablis, since, if it is exposed to wood, it will lose all its freshness and youthful fruit with the premature ageing that occurs in wood. Accordingly, companies like J. Moreau et Fils ferment and store their wine in stainless steel vats, or, if they cannot afford these, concrete vats lined with enamel or fibreglass. Some also store their wine under a blanket of carbon dioxide, to ensure that there is no possibility of any oxygen penetrating the wine.

At the other extreme is a man like William Fèvre, who built a new cellar in 1979 that contains nothing but new oak barrels. All his wine spends four to five months in new oak, and his barrels are changed every four years, since he considers that, after that period, they become ineffective, as by then they are coated in tartrate crystals. Fèvre believes that the natural aromas of a wine develop better in wood than in vat, as a result of the slow, almost imperceptible oxidation process, and that the new wood gives complementary aromas to the wine. In addition, if the wine rests in wood over several months, it will clarify naturally, thus removing the need to filter it to excess.

Somewhere mid-way between these two points of view is Michel Laroche. His company has all the modern equipment needed for the making of wine, but he feels, like Gérard Vuillien of Long Depaquit, that there may be an argument for returning to the ageing of *grands crus*, and possibly *premiers crus*, in oak. His experiments, however, have been very tentative and on a small scale. He has bought a small quantity of new oak barrels from the Allier and is ageing some *grands* and *premiers crus* in these for about three months; he will compare the results with wine from the same vineyard that has seen no oak. Laroche is very anxious, and rightly, to avoid the pronounced vanilla oak flavour that is typical of so many Californian Chardonnays. Much depends on the basic structure of the wine; it needs a wine with a certain initial weight and character to benefit from ageing in new oak. For instance, it was interesting to compare the effects of oak on a 1981 Blanchot, and the same wine when made solely from thirty-five-year-old vines. The wine from the older vines was much better able to absorb the oak influence than the wine from the younger vines. The character of an individual vintage is also significant; a rich year, like 1978 or 1981, is better suited to ageing in wood than a lighter year of less substance, such as 1980.

Then there are a number of small growers who carry on using the same oak *feuillettes* that they have always used ever since they have been making wine. Louis Pinson is one such grower; in contrast to William Fèvre, he does not believe that the effect of wood diminishes with the use of old barrels, but that new barrels are unsuitable for Chablis, as they will make the wine too tannic. However, oak barrels, of whatever age, allow the subtle process of oxidation by which the wine develops. François Raveneau and René Dauvissat also firmly believe in the use of wood: that oak ageing makes a wine that will mature more slowly and last longer – in other words, a very much better wine. The average age of the barrels in Raveneau's cellars is twenty years; of those in Dauvissat's cellars, ten years. After Fèvre, Dauvissat probably has a higher proportion of new barrels than any other grower in Chablis. Some growers, like Luc Michaut, use both vats and barrels, blending their wine together before bottling. Others, although basically not in favour of wood, still keep a few old barrels to use when they have run out of vat space, or when they just have a small quantity of a wine which does not justify storing in a large vat.

Three considerable disadvantages arise from the use of the oak barrel: expense, hygiene and the complicated handling operations which are entailed. New oak barrels cost between 1,000 and 1,500 francs – a substantial outlay when several have to be purchased at one time. The risk of a fault occurring in the wine is also greater with the use of wood. Empty barrels have to be very carefully looked after and treated with sulphur before reuse. The hygiene must be absolutely faultless, or else considerable harm can come to the wine, with the risk of an off-taste coming from a dirty barrel. Also, with the disappearance of the craft of the *tonnelier* it has become increasingly difficult to maintain wooden barrels. Other drawbacks are that barrels take up more space in a small cellar and are cumbersome to move – as they have to be moved when the wine is racked. Moreover, the 'angels' share' of wine that has evaporated through the wood has to be replaced, for a *feuillette* will absorb two to three litres of wine during the first month of use and at least a half-litre in each subsequent month. The barrels therefore need to be topped up every month in an operation known as *ouillage*.

Variations between barrels of the same wine in the same cellar are apparent; there is greater individuality and less uniformity with oak barrels. These differences, however, are immaterial, since the wine will be blended together before bottling.

To use wood, or not to use wood, is the most significant factor to influence the different styles of Chablis. But another important factor is the length of time the wine is aged before bottling, be it in oak or in vat. This can vary considerably, and the decision is also influenced by the quality of the wine, be it simple Chablis or *grand cru* Chablis. For instance, Paul Droin keeps his *grands crus* in wood for twelve months, whereas his *premiers crus* (which he does not feel are complex enough for wood ageing) are bottled after six months in vat.

A traditional grower, like François Raveneau or René Dauvissat, will keep his wine in vat until the malolactic fermentation has occurred and then, in the spring following the vintage, transfer it into barrel, where it will remain for a further twelve months.

When I saw Raveneau in May 1981 he was just about to begin bottling his 1979s. At the other end of the scale, Alain Geoffroy, who aims to make young fresh Chablis for early sale, had already bottled his 1981 Beauroy in May 1982. This was a wine that had only spent a few months in vat. Somewhere in the middle are people like Michel Rémon, who use very little wood, but still believe that, if Chablis is bottled too young, its quality is adversely affected and that it will make a 'vin trop primeur'. A great deal depends on the character and quality of the individual wine. Its evolution must be followed and this can vary from vat to vat or barrel to barrel and from wine to wine and vintage to vintage. However it can also be a question of expediency: of bottling when there is an order for a wine, or in time to house the next vintage.

Other treatments of the wine are possible, depending on the growers' individual preferences. Many, like Louis Michel, aim to make their wine as simply and as naturally as possible, with the minimum amount of treatment. The wine will be racked after the malolactic fermentation, when it is transferred into a barrel or vat. Those who keep their wine in wood will probably rack it twice during the year. Those who keep their wine in vat will fine it, most commonly with bentonite, or with casein. All will filter their wine before bottling. The *négociants* are equipped with large automatic bottling lines and often bottle under inert gas to prevent any possible risk of oxidation. Some of the smaller growers, who sell only in bottle, have their own less sophisticated machines, and many, who only sell a small proportion of their wine in bottle, depend upon the services of a mobile bottling machine that comes from Mâcon or Beaune.

Since 1978 Chablis, in common with many other French wines, has been subject to compulsory tastings and analysis. This is a measure designed to guarantee the quality of a wine with an appellation and to ensure that the wine merits its label. The *labellisation* tastings, as they are therefore known, are held under the auspices of the INAO. The tasting commission is chosen by a Union Intersyndicale, made up of members of the two *syndicats* of growers, who select about thirty tasters. *Agents de prélèvement* take samples from each grower's cellars at the beginning of December and the wine is tasted shortly afterwards. In 1980, sixteen wines were rejected at the first tasting, but if they were suffering from a curable malady, they could be submitted for a second tasting six months later. Jean Durup believes that these tastings have had a beneficial effect on the quality of Chablis and that the growers, as a result of them, are forced to take greater care of their wine. William Fèvre is more sceptical, describing the system as a farce, for only one sample is taken from each cellar, regardless of how many different wines a grower may make. When the wine is approved, it is given a *bulletin d'agrément*, which allows it to be offered for sale and moved from a grower's cellar.

So what then in the end is really good Chablis? What is it that gives Chablis that indefinable taste of gunflint, its steely acidity and ethereal fruit and flavour? Its basic character undoubtedly comes from the unique combination of soil and grape variety, but the role of the winemaker is vital in determining the quality of the wine. Hygiene is obviously essential: nothing is more detrimental to a wine than dirty cellars. But above all, it is the love and care that a grower gives to his wine that counts. With the development of alternatives to oak ageing have come almost two contrasting styles of Chablis: the young, fresh, almost flowery wine that has seen no wood, and the fuller, more complex, oak-aged wine. It is impossible to say that one is better than the other; it depends upon a subjective decision of personal taste. The following chapter on the different growers offers some guidance as to who does what.

François Raveneau pouring a tasting sample in his delightfully old-fashioned cellars

5
WHO'S WHO: THE ORGANIZATION OF THE CHABLIS MARKET AND THE DIFFERENT PRODUCERS

The main part of this chapter offers a guide to the principal producers of Chablis. It covers all the *négociants* and all the growers who bottle at least some of their own wine. It contains accounts of all those whom I have visited and whose wine (in nearly every case) I have tasted. In addition, I have attempted to compile a list of the names of all the other growers who sell their wine in bottle, whose name can be found on a Chablis label, but whom I have not visited.

To establish a complete list of all the growers in Chablis, including all those who either sell to the *négoce* or belong to the co-operative, is an enterprise fraught with hazard. It is true that every grower must declare his annual production at the town hall and the *déclaration des rendements* is available for any interested party to see. However, parcels of vine-yards ostensibly cultivated by the same man may be under the name of his wife, his father-in-law or his son, and there are several families with the same surname who may, or may not, be related. Moreover, there is not just one list of growers in the *mairie* in Chablis; there are twenty separate lists, one for each village. Nor would a list of the members of the two *syndicats* of growers give a complete picture, as there are growers, some of considerable importance, who have withdrawn from membership of either *syndicat*. Somebody once said that the only complete list of wine growers in any part of France is in the local telephone directory. I even have doubts about that, since not everyone is on the telephone in this provincial backwater. So I can only apologize for any omissions.

First, however, it will be helpful to outline briefly the organization of the Chablis market. In the 1930s commerce depended upon the *commissionaires*, whose role was that of intermediaries between the growers and the *négociants* of the Côte d'Or and Bordeaux, the wine merchants of Paris and, before the delimitation of the production area of Champagne, the *négociants* of the Marne. The *commissionaire* selected wines for the *négociants* and carried out any necessary treatments on their behalf until the wine was ready for delivery in *feuillette*. Sales were always made by the *feuillette* of 132 litres and included the oak barrel itself.

At this stage, *vente directe* – that is, the sale of wine in bottle to private individuals, often unconnected with the trade, who come directly to the grower's cellar door – was already beginning. Writing in the 1930s, Albert Pic[1] notes how some of the Paris restaurants preferred to come direct to Chablis, rather than go through the *négociants* of the Haute Bourgogne; he comments that they may be saving money that way, but that this is at the expense of the trade of the Côte d'Or. He also notices the number of amateurs who prefer to buy their fine wine in bottle, direct from the area of production, as a surer guarantee of authenticity. This is a trend that is growing today.

For nearly thirty years there was little change, but the market has greatly changed over the past twenty years or so. According to William Fèvre, in 1960 75 per cent of all Chablis was sold through Beaune, the other *négociants* of Burgundy, and through Bordeaux. The Chablis *négoce* accounted for 20 per cent of the production and a mere 5 per cent was sold by the growers themselves. Today the picture is different. The Beaune *négoce*, together with companies from the Saône et Loire, Bordeaux and Paris, sell 50 per cent; the Chablis *négoce* has increased its share to 35–40 per cent and the growers now account for 10–15 per cent of the Chablis market. In the context of these figures it is hard to give an exact indication of the importance of the Chablisienne co-operative (see below), since this sells not only under its own label and under various members' names, but also in bulk to *négociants* in Beaune and Chablis, as well as abroad in bulk and bottle. These figures do, however, illustrate the changing role and increasing importance of the Chablis *négoce*, compared to its Beaune counterparts, and a similar growth in the activity of the small growers. To deal with the Chablis *négoce* first, Michel Rémon, of A. Régnard et Fils, remembers that, when he began in 1947, 80 per cent of his work was that of a broker, or *commissionaire*, for the *négociants* of Beaune. The scales have now turned, so that the Beaune *négociants* find their own wines, and the Chablis *négociants* work only as *négociants* for Chablis and the surrounding vineyards of the Yonne.

Traditionally, as I have mentioned, Chablis was sold by the *feuillette*; the *négociant* tasted a grower's wine when it was barely finished in the

---

[1] *Le Vignoble de Chablis.*

late autumn and made his decision to purchase *sur place*. Today the tendency is for the *négociants* to buy must from the growers, with some of whom they have long-term contracts. In this way the *négociants* can be confident of the quality of their wines, in that they make the wine that they sell under their own name and have complete responsibility for the results. The general assumption that a grower's wine will be better than a *négociant*'s wine is unfounded – although it may be. The growers may know all there is to be known about producing grapes, but the experience of many of them of wine-making is limited. For many of them wine-making is a new activity and their equipment can be unsatisfactory and inadequate.

In Chablis today there are about ten growers who sell all their wine in bottle under their own name, but about 20–30 per cent who sell some in bottle and the remainder – possibly the greater part – to the *négociants* of Beaune and Chablis. It is only since the war that the growers have acquired this independence; with the advent of the tractor the average family's vineyard holding has increased, and with effective methods of frost protection has come a confidence in their ability to make a living out of their wines.

Some of the small growers reproach the *négociants*, be they of Beaune or Chablis, for the severe price fluctuations and swings in the market situation. 'La négoce, elle fait la pluie et le beau temps' was a comment that was made to me on more than one occasion. So the growers see the success of the *négociants* on the export market and want to try their luck too; they are able to take advantage of the growing trend to buy Chablis from Chablis itself, rather than elsewhere. Many have also built up a private clientèle as *vente directe* becomes a more common practice.

One may be forgiven for wondering whether the Beaune *négoce* has suffered with the acquisition of confidence by the Chablis growers. In fact, although its share of the market has fallen, the quantity of wine which it handles has not changed dramatically, as this has coincided with a significant increase in production. Only two Beaune *négociants* own any vineyards in the Chablisien; they are Joseph Drouhin and Albert Bichot et Cie, both of whom are mentioned below.

The *négociants* and growers are discussed below in three sections, each in alphabetical order: (1) the co-operative, La Chablisienne, followed by *négociants* in Chablis; (2) *négociants* outside Chablis; (3) the growers of Chablis itself; (4) the growers of other villages. A final section lists the names of growers whom I have not visited and who are not discussed individually in the previous four sections. Fyé, Rameau and Poilly-sur-Serein are excluded from (4), as there are no growers with cellars in these villages, and Viviers likewise, as the vineyards of Viviers are owned by Bichot and Moreau, who are listed in their own right.

La Chablisienne and Négociants in Chablis

LA CHABLISIENNE

The co-operative known as La Chablisienne accounts for nearly a third of the total production of Chablis, with a membership of 189 growers, whose vineyards range in size from one to twenty hectares, with eight hectares being the average. Their names are listed in Appendix 10.

La Chablisienne was founded in 1923, at a time when the Chablis market was in a state of crisis. The growers were unable to sell their wine or to make a living; in 1919 a *feuillette* was offered at 550 francs, but was not sold until two or three years later, when the price had halved. La Chablisienne is one of the earliest wine co-operatives in France. It was the idea of three local personages: Abbé Balitran (the *curé* of Poinchy), Fernand Poinsot (an *administrateur délégué*, or civil servant) and M. Persenoud (a retired school teacher). All three were doubtless inspired by the ideals of the co-operative movement.

From 1923 until 1947 the co-operative existed essentially to help the growers sell the wine that they made in their own cellars. However, it suffered a severe setback when in 1929 Poinsot and the *curé* quarrelled over policy and over the relationship of the co-operative to the *négociants*, with the result that eventually, in 1934, all the growers who supported the *curé* withdrew from the co-operative, leaving it with only fifty growers. The existing stocks were sold at auction to the *négociants* at very low prices.

The fortunes of La Chablisienne took a definite turn for the better with the arrival of M. Fortin as director in 1947. He arranged the installation of a vinification plant – which, in the post-war period, greatly helped the widows who were running many of the vineyards and who were unable to cope with making their own wine as well. Since then the growers have always brought their crop to the co-operative in the form of must, and to this day La Chablisienne does not have a press. Its methods are those of a classic white wine vinification – with, however, a tendency to over-chaptalize. There are no wooden barrels and only modern equipment is used. Storage capacity now amounts to sixty thousand hectolitres, since new vats were built to house the large 1979 vintage. The two rather lurid brown, light-green- and dark-green-striped vats, that seem to tower above the co-operative's buildings, have been described by another producer as 'bonbons anglais' – a compliment to English sweets, perhaps?

Once a grower has joined La Chablisienne, the terms of entry are such that it is extremely difficult for him to withdraw; otherwise, the tendency would be for him to take refuge under the co-operative's wing in hard times and reassume independence in good times, which would disrupt the efficiency of its organization and running. There was an increase in membership during the 1970s, when conditions in the trade were not easy. In theory, it would be possible for the co-operative to refuse admission, but in practice this has never happened.

The value of the vintage is decided by a Conseil d'Administration, and each grower is paid accordingly, with a bonus if the quality is finer than average. The final payment is not made until the entire vintage has been sold. Although the growers run their vineyards independently, they can turn to the co-operative for help and advice over any problems that may occur.

The present director of La Chablisienne, Jean-Michel Tucki, describes its house style as 'tout à fait honnête' and representative of Chablis from all parts of the region, for the members of the co-operative do indeed come from all twenty communes of the vineyard. The members' vineyards total some 472 hectares; all the *grands crus* except Valmur are represented. The fifteen hectares of *grands crus* include the part of Grenouilles that belonged to the Testut family and which is now run by a Groupement Agricole d'Exploitation en Commun (GAEC) – an association of seven members of the co-operative. Of the *premiers crus* Fourchaume is the most important, with 35 out of 97 hectares; simple Chablis accounts for 310 hectares and Petit Chablis 50 hectares.

Apart from wines sold under the La Chablisienne label, the co-operative's wines are found under any of the 189 members' names. This use, or rather misuse, of a member's name is very confusing for the consumer – and, indeed, even morally reprehensible. For the mention, for example, of 'Henri Dupas, viticulteur à Fontenay-près-Chablis' on a label implies that the wine in the bottle was made by M. Dupas at his cellar in Fontenay, whereas, in fact, it came out of the communal co-operative vat.

However, only 10 per cent of the co-operative's production is sold in bottle. By far the greater proportion is sold in bulk: 20 per cent to other

Chablis *négociants* and 70 per cent to *négociants* in Beaune and elsewhere in France and on the export market.

Henri Laroche

The activities of the company of Henri Laroche are based on the considerable vineyard holdings of the Laroche family, amounting to some eighty-one hectares. These have grown from small beginnings. Jean-Victor Laroche was an *ouvrier viticulteur* at Maligny in the 1850s, and even two generations later the family owned no more than four hectares of vines. It was the present head of the family, Henri Laroche, and his son Michel who were responsible for the expansion of the

Michel Laroche sampling his Chablis

family property. In addition to Domaine Laroche, Domaine La Jouchère was created, initially as a separate *domaine*; from January 1982 the two *domaines* were formed into a combined property and Domaine La Jouchère is now used as a *sous marque*. There is also the *négociant* company of Bacheroy Josselin, which exists to complement the family's own production of Chablis and deals in the other red and white wines of the Yonne, as well as those of the Côte d'Or and Mâconnais.

Blanchot, Les Clos and Bougros form the basis of their *grands crus*; in the *premier cru* category they own some Fourchaume, Montmains, Vaillons and Beauroy, as well as a newly planted *premier cru* at Beines called Vaudevey, which came into production for the first time in 1983.

Henri Laroche have modern installations at Beines and Milly and a more traditional cellar at Maligny. Apart from some experimental ageing of *grands crus* in new oak *feuillettes*, they are very modern in their methods and techniques. Cultured yeasts are used, the must is treated by a centrifuge and the fermentation temperature is closely controlled. The result is very good: a light, fresh Chablis, with plenty of fruit, but lacking the weight of some of the traditionally oak-aged Chablis.

The company is now run by Michel Laroche, a tall man in his forties – cold, handsome and with a quiet confidence in the quality of his wines. He lives in one of Chablis' older and finer houses, the Obédiencerie, on the site of which the monastery of Saint Loup originally stood, as I mentioned in my first chapter. The cellars are the oldest part of the house and may well have sheltered the body of Saint Martin. Today they house Michel Laroche's pristine new oak barrels. Across the courtyard there is a magnificent fourteenth-century press.

An original marketing exercise (undertaken with the restaurant trade in mind) was the introduction in 1982 of Chablis '50': Chablis sold in 50-centilitre bottles. It is apparently proving a popular idea. The wines of Henri Laroche are also sold under the *sous marque* names of Henri Josset, Ferdinand Bacheroy, Jacques Millar, Jean Baulat, Roland Foucard, Paul Dupressoir and Alain Combard.

J. Moreau et Fils

To think of Chablis, many people would say, is to think of Moreau, for his is the best known name in the Chablis market. His wine is sold in nearly all the wine-drinking countries of the world, from the West Indies to Hong Kong, by way of North America and Great Britain. His reputation is due, not only to Chablis, but also to a white table wine, Moreau Blanc.

In 1814, the year before the Battle of Waterloo, Jean Joseph Moreau arrived in Chablis from Montbard, near Dijon, where he had been a *tonnelier*. Out of work there, he sought pastures new in Chablis and his subsequent marriage to a Mlle Ducard, whose father was a *vigneron*, led to the founding of the Moreau-Ducard company. The Moreaus continued to marry well. Jean Joseph's son, Alexandre, married a Mlle Riotte, whose father was a wealthy vineyard-owner, and their son married a Mlle Guenier, whose father was similarly well endowed. Thus the foundations of a successful enterprise were laid. The family house in Chablis had been bought in 1830 as well as parcels of Les Clos and Vaudésir.

Today the present head of the company, Jean Jacques Moreau, is the largest vineyard-owner in Chablis, with property amounting to seventy hectares. His seven hectares of Les Clos include the Clos des Hospices, a small parcel of land that belonged to the hospital of Chablis until it was bought by the Moreau family in 1850. He also has two hectares of Valmur and small parcels of Vaudésir and Blanchot in *grand crus*, ten hectares of Vaillons in *premier cru* and a recently created vineyard of fifty hectares of Chablis at Viviers called Domaine de Biéville. In addition to the production of his own vineyards, he buys must from other growers to supplement his requirements.

Moreau is essentially a white wine expert, rather than a Chablis specialist. He deals in more than sixty white wines of the different French appellations and in 1978 introduced a branded table wine, Moreau Blanc, whose success is growing. However, possibly as a result of the distinctive Moreau labels, there has been in some minds, in some markets, a definite confusion between Moreau Blanc and Moreau Chablis. Moreau Blanc is, in the words of a letter from Jean Jacques Moreau himself, 'a blend of French *vins de table*, coming from the northern vineyards of France. There is not one drop of *appellation contrôlée* white wine and furthermore no Chablis wine in it. The breakdown of the blend is partly Chardonnay, Chenin and Sauvignon *vins de table*' – presumably from somewhere around the Loire valley. To partner the white, there is a Moreau Rouge of southern provenance.

Although Moreau is the oldest company in Chablis, with an appropriate sense of tradition, the new vinification plant – some unkindly call it a factory – is the most modern. Not for him are oak barrels and a lengthy maturation; concrete and stainless steel are the norm and the result is a young, fruity wine, with the individual Moreau style – which you may, or may not, like. A storage capacity of sixty thousand hectolitres makes him the largest *négociant* of Chablis, and although his vineyards are his family property, 50 per cent of his *négociant* company is owned by Hiram Walker.

Virtually all Moreau's wine is sold on the export market and most of it under his own name, but his *sous marques* include Petits Fils de Guenier, Alexandre de Ghislain, Paul Ferrand, Paul Vollereau, Philibert Ducard and Adolphe Hélie.

Jean Jacques Moreau himself is one of Chablis' more dynamic wine-makers. A man in his forties, he exudes energy and confidence, and he usually sports a healthy suntan, even in midwinter, as he holidays at his second home in Guadeloupe. Nevertheless, diversification of his range of wines and the introduction of a branded wine are an indication of his perhaps pessimistic view of the future of the Chablis market. Certainly he has planned with foresight, and with a greater awareness than many of his competitors of more limited vision, for a future that may be difficult.

A. Régnard et Fils

A. Régnard et Fils (founded in 1860) are the only *négociants* in Chablis not to have any vineyards of their own. However, their list encompasses the whole range of Chablis – *premiers* and *grands crus* and simple Chablis – as well as some Aligoté and Sauvignon de Saint Bris. They also make and bottle the wine from the thirty ares of Vaudésir which belong to Peter Reynier, of the London shippers, J. B. Reynier; this vineyard was bought by Peter Reynier's father Joseph in the 1930s.

The company of A. Régnard is run by the very likeable and energetic Michel Rémon (Régnard is his wife's family). He is enthusiastically generous with his wines. I remember tasting the whole range of his 1978 *grands crus*, among others, in the cellar of his house in the rue d'Auxerre. He views his wines with a refreshing objectivity and is quite prepared to point out their faults as well as their virtues. He is also that rare Frenchman who is unchauvinistic enough to enjoy wines from outside his own region, and claret is one of his passions. His wines are sold not only under his own name and the company name, but also under the well known Chablis name of Albert Pic, which goes back to 1755. After the last member of the Pic family died in the 1930s, the company was run by a brother-in-law, until it was bought by Régnard in 1957.

Although Michel Rémon has a few oak barrels, through which some of his wine will pass for a maximum of three months, he prefers

Michel Rémon in the cellars of his house in the rue Auxerroise

stainless steel. Otherwise, his methods are traditional; he is against bottling his wine too early, as he believes that this devalues its quality, and his wines are a good example of classic Chablis that is widely available in Britain.

Simmonet-Febvre

The present head of the company, which was founded in 1840, is Jean-Claude Simmonet. His great-great-grandfather (M. Febvre) worked for a M. Tisserand, who made sparkling wines which he sold as champagne – under the name of Moët and Chandon, to be precise – in bottles bearing labels which he had had printed in Chablis. One day,

Bottles in an old-fashioned automatic *remuage* machine in Simmonet-Febvre's cellars

one of his customers, an Englishman who was 'un peu plus voleur que lui', decided not to pay him, and, unable to take legal action, he was faced with bankruptcy. M. Febvre took the opportunity to buy his equipment at a bargain price and went into business, selling his wine under his own name. His only child – a daughter, Amédée – married a M. Simmonet, and it was thus that the company acquired its double-barrelled name.

They have a few vineyards of their own: two hectares of Chablis, 1.5 hectares of Mont de Milieu and 1.5 hectares of Preuses. However, as *négociants éleveurs*, they buy must and deal in a wide range of *crus*, the most important being Montée de Tonnerre, Mont de Milieu, Four-chaume and Vaillons. In accordance with their origins, they also produce a sparkling wine, Bourgogne Mousseux, made by the *méthode champenoise*, but although the appellation is destined to be replaced by Crémant de Bourgogne, for the moment they are still allowed to use the term. They are the only people in Chablis to make a sparkling wine. Other growers sometimes supply them with wine for this purpose, which they then take back to sell under their own label; but the total production is very small. However, their cellars contain some extra-ordinary forerunners of the automatic *remuers* to be found in the modern champagne cellars of Reims and Epernay. They also have some excellent Irancy and Coulanges-la-Vineuse.

Although they are not in favour of oak ageing, they do in fact have some old cellars containing casks of Tronçais oak that are over a hundred years old. However, these are only used when the stock situation demands it. Generally, Jean-Claude Simmonet likes to bottle his wines young, so that the consumer can age them in bottle himself.

Simmonet is a friendly man and an enthusiastic member of the Piliers Chablisiens (see p. 119), with an appropriate sense of humour where the organization of their *intronisation* ceremonies is concerned. His cousin, Jean Pierre Simmonet, is also involved with the running of the company.

Apart from the Simmonet-Febvre label, the company's wines are sold under the names of Jean-Claude Simmonet, André Vannier, Jean Deligny, Georges Martin, Alexandre Gourland and Gilles Blanchard.

Négociants outside Chablis

Joseph Drouhin

Apart from Bichot, Joseph Drouhin is the only Côte d'Or company to own vineyards in Chablis. These have been gradually acquired since 1969 and consist of Les Clos, Vaudésir and Preuses in *grands crus*, seven hectares of *premiers crus* made up of tiny parcels from an assortment of different vineyards (the wine being all blended together without a vineyard name) and seventeen hectares of simple Chablis. Their wine is a light, fruity style of Chablis, the result of ageing some wine in wood, some in vat, and then blending both wines. It is all vinified and bottled at Beaune.

Patrick de Ladoucette

Most of the outside interest in Chablis comes from Beaune and the Saône et Loire; less from *négociants* in Bordeaux. Baron Patrick de Ladoucette is the only producer on the Loire to show any interest in Chablis. This is not really surprising, for he is a white wine specialist par excellence and his properties in Sancerre and Pouilly-sur-Loire are not so very far from Chablis. An attempt to purchase some land in Chablis was foiled by the SAFER. He now buys wine from the growers, like any other *négociant*; it is then entrusted to one company for its *élevage* and bottling in Chablis, before it is sent to Sancerre. It is to be found mainly on the American market, under the label of Baron Patrick.

Growers in Chablis

Domaine Billaud-Simon et Fils

Jean Billaud's establishment is to be found behind tall walls at the end of the Quai de Reugny, overlooking the Serein. You have to walk through the vegetable gardens behind the house before you get to his rather disorganized but quite modern cellars. Jean Billaud's grandfather, M. Simon, owned small parcels of Les Clos, Vaudésir and Mont de Milieu. The property, increased by Jean's father and himself, now includes Preuses and Blanchot in *grands crus* and Montée de Tonnerre and Vaillons in *premiers crus*. He still has fifteen hectares of simple Chablis to plant, which he is doing little by little each year.

He mainly uses enamel-lined vats, in which his wine is kept for twelve to fifteen months, depending on demand. There are also a few old barrels, through which his wine might pass for three or four months. In 1954 he began bottling his wine, following a demand from America, and before the price rises of the 1970s he sold all his wine in bottle to the United States. The situation is now improving again, but he still sells half his wine to the Chablis *négoce*.

A tasting of his 1981s from vat, and of some 1980s, gave an overriding impression of austerity – of elegant wines, with a good steely bite.

Jean Collet et Fils

Jean Collet, a wine-maker well respected in Chablis, is the Grand Architrave of the Piliers Chablisiens and a man of a stature appropriate to this title. As another grower remarked, 'C'est un monument.' Unfortunately, when it comes to trying to see him about his wines, he becomes maddeningly elusive and I have never succeeded in tracking him down. However, a bottle of 1978 Montmains, shared with friends in London when it was five years old, had all the finesse of a great Chablis, with the characteristic *pierre à fusil* flavour. Collet's twenty-one hectare *domaine* consists mainly of *premiers crus* (Vaillons and Montmains being the most important), as well as some simple Chablis. He is one of the few growers who still ferments in oak *foudres*.

René Dauvissat working in his cellars in Chablis

René Dauvissat

René Dauvissat is small but beautiful; his six hectares include Forêts, Séchet and Vaillons in *premiers crus* and Les Clos and Preuses in *grands crus*. All are sold under his own name.

Dauvissat belongs to the traditional school, that keep their wine in oak for several months before bottling (so that the tartrates fall naturally during the winter months), and he favours the moderate use of new oak barrels. When I met him in May 1981, we talked while he and his wife bottled, and I tasted, their 1979 Preuses – and very good it was, too. He is a shy, unassuming man, rather serious, with a quiet confidence in his work.

René Dauvissat's great-grandfather began as a *tonnelier* with a few vines; it was his grandfather who began to develop the vineyard. Today it is very much a small family business, which he runs with his son, selling mainly to exclusive restaurants in Paris and a little on the export market. He and François Raveneau are the only two growers to continue to use wax capsules for their bottles; they keep the bottles really air-tight, so that the maturation process is gentle and gradual.

Paul Droin et Fils

Paul Droin's great-grandfather presented his wines to Napoleon III as he passed through Auxerre in 1866. His father married a *vigneron's* daughter, and now the family vineyards amount to fourteen hectares, which he runs with his son, Jean Paul. Droin is one of the five principal owners of Grenouilles and also has parcels of Les Clos, Valmur and Vaudésir. Some Montée de Tonnerre, Vaillons and Montmains account for about seven hectares of *premiers crus*, together with 2.5 hectares of simple Chablis. His small cellar contains old oak barrels for the *grands crus*, which are bottled after twelve months in wood. The *premiers crus*, which do not see any wood, spend six months in vat. I owe my first taste of Grenouilles to Paul Droin's enthusiastic hospitality; the 1980 vintage, tasted from cask in July 1981, had very good fruit – a lovely, buttery Chardonnay flavour, with balancing acidity and a long finish.

Marcel Duplessis

Marcel Duplessis is a very small grower and very typical of traditional attitudes. I suspect that the outside world tends to pass him by. He said I could come and see him if it was raining, for then he would not be working 'dans la vigne'. His family have been *viticulteurs* for four generations and he now has five hectares, made up of small pockets of Les Clos, Montée de Tonnerre, Montmains, Fourchaume and Vaillons. He keeps his wine in *cuve* for six months and in wood for a year. I have been told that the quality of his wines can be good, but is sometimes a little erratic.

William Fèvre

The first thing I asked William Fèvre when we met, was why he had an English Christian name. He replied that in the late nineteenth century it was considered rather chic to give one's children English Christian names, and that he was named after an uncle who was killed in the First World War at about the time he was born. The Fèvres are an old-established Chablis family who have been *viticulteurs* since the reign of Louis XV. They originated from Fontenay-près-Chablis and in the early 1800s the family accounted for half the population of that village. Today the family and business occupy a rather impressive building in the rue Jules Rathier. The building in fact belonged to the Rathiers, a notable Chablis family who were involved in viticulture, local and even national politics throughout the nineteenth century. Jules Rathier, who was Mayor of Chablis in 1870, was responsible for the building of the existing house, in its neo-renaissance style of the 1880s.

William Fèvre is the largest owner of *grands crus* Chablis; his sixteen hectares include parcels of them all, except Blanchot. He also has a wide

William Fèvre, president of the Syndicat de la Défence de l'Appellation de Chablis and owner of Domaine de la Maladière

selection of *premiers crus* and ordinary Chablis, and his total holding amounts to some twenty-five hectares.

He is the exponent par excellence of the use of new oak and in 1979 built a very impressive new cellar, which is filled with new oak barrels, purchased from Nuits St Georges. His wines, when young, have the characteristic flavour of new oak, but this is tempered as they mature. They are sold not only under his own name, but more often under that of Domaine de la Maladière, a name that originates from a corruption of the name of the old leprosy hospital at Chablis, Maladrerie.

As mentioned in an earlier chapter, Fèvre is the protagonist of 'le vrai Chablis'. He fervently believes in the importance of 'le kimmeridgien' and sincerely considers that the quality of Chablis has suffered with the extension of the vineyard in a 'manière anarchique'. As well as being a winemaker, he was also a student at the Ecole Nationale d'Administration. He is now also a civil servant and one of France's forty Contrôleurs d'Etat, responsible for the financial control of Sociétés d'Autoroutes.

Raoul Gautherin et Fils

The family *domaine*, created by Raoul Gautherin, now consists of 1.35 hectares of *grands crus* in Vaudésir, Les Clos and Grenouilles, and ten hectares of *premiers crus*, of which Montmains and Vaillons are the most important.. There are also two hectare-sized parcels of Chablis at Chemilly-sur-Serein and Chablis. I met Raoul Gautherin's son Alain, who was fresh from oenology studies in Beaune and was refreshing in his approach to the 'establishment' of Chablis.

The *domaine* seems like an estate in transition: they ferment in both *foudres* and *fûts*. *Foudres* are better, as it is easier to control the temperature of a larger container. However, in 1982 they installed vats, which are more practical, and refrigerated their wine for the first time. Otherwise, they aim to treat their wine as little as possible, after which they store it for ten months in old barrels.

They differ from many of the small growers in Chablis in that the domestic market is important for them, and they can sell in bulk to Beaune. However, they also export to Germany and Belgium.

Domaine A. Long Depaquit

The origins of the Long Depaquit family are related under Société Civile de la Moutonne (q.v.). After the death of the last direct descendant of the Long Depaquit family in 1967 a company was created with the financial backing of the Beaune *négociants*, Bichot, with Albert Bichot and other members of the company as shareholders. However, the estate is run autonomously under the control of its competent *régisseur*, Gérard Vuillien.

Apart from a sizeable portion of La Moutonne, the estate has been expanded to include 10 per cent of the *grands crus* Blanchot, Preuses, Les Clos and Vaudésir. In *premiers crus* they own some Vaillons (including Beugnon and Les Lys) and Vaucoupin and about ten hectares of simple Chablis.

The cellars of Long Depaquit are situated around an attractive courtyard off the rue d'Auxerre; they were modernized in 1973, but still retain an aura of tradition, with their old vaults. The wine is made with great care; some of the ordinary Chablis is bottled by Bichot in Beaune,

The Domaine of Long Depaquit, which dominates a courtyard in the main street of Chablis

but all the *grands* and *premiers crus* are bottled in Chablis. This wine is sold partly under the name of Long Depaquit and partly under the name of Bichot and the company's various *sous marques*.

Louis Michel

Louis Michel has a quiet confidence in the quality of his wines – and rightly. For some they are among the best that Chablis has to offer. His is a family business: his father and grandfather were both *viticulteurs*, and he himself has increased his holding from five to eighteen hectares. He now works with his son, Jean-Loup. *Premiers crus* predominate, with considerable portions of Montmains, Montée de Tonnerre, Vaillons and Forêts and a little Fourchaume. Michel is also one of the principal owners of Grenouilles and has a little Vaudésir and Les Clos, as well as a couple of hectares of simple Chablis.

No wood is used; Michel does make a *vin de garde*, but the ageing is in stainless-steel vats, after a carefully controlled fermentation, and generally he aims to work his wine as little as possible. The results are superb: wines of elegance and depth, without being overpowering, such as the 1978 Grenouilles tasted in July 1981. His wine is sold either under his own name or under the recently created label Domaine de la Tour Vaubourg, a reference to the ivy-covered tower that forms part of the house. The basic vineyards for this label are owned by Jean-Loup but run as a GAEC.

Société Civile de la Moutonne

The vineyard of La Moutonne belonged to the monks of Pontigny until the sale of their property after the French Revolution. At that time it consisted of 1.11 hectares of the *climat* of Vaudésir – so called because, in the words of the monks, it was 'pissatif et léger, faict sauter le buveur comme un petit mouton'. Another theory about the origin of the name was that the wine was light, with diuretic properties that likened a man to a sheep rather than a lion.

When the monastic vineyards were sold in 1791, they were bought initially by a M. Mignard, and immediately afterwards passed over to Simon Depaquit, the former *procureur* (procurator) of the abbey. His descendants, who subsequently became the family of Long Depaquit (q.v.), looked after La Moutonne and increased their vineyards during the nineteenth century. Curiously, La Moutonne is not mentioned either by Jullien in 1816, or by Rendu in 1857, but Dr Guyot cites it as one of the best Chablis *crus* in 1868. Since then the status of Moutonne has been subject to some confusion. Although it is a recognized vineyard site on the slopes of the *grands crus*, it is not one of the seven *grands crus* of the appellation. At one time Moutonne was used by the Long Depaquit family as a commercial brand name to cover not only wine from the original monastic vineyards, but also others owned by the family. However, in 1950 an agreement was made with the INAO, limiting la Moutonne to the production of 2.35 hectares of the vineyards of Preuses and Vaudésir. Although the INAO was prepared to consider the acceptance of a separate *grand cru*, this was never realized.

The vineyards remained the property of the Long Depaquit family until 1967, when the direct line died out. A *société civile* was then created, so that 82.5 per cent now belongs to Albert Bichot and 17.5 per cent to Joseph Drouhin. Philippe Testut, who worked on the estate when he first came to Chablis in the 1960s, has a small share in the production.

La Moutonne is not often found; the production is very small, but it is worth seeking out.

Louis Pinson

Louis Pinson and his wife are welcoming and hospitable. 'On va toute suite à la cave' – so we did, and a bottle of 1979 Forêts was opened. Pinson's cellars are old, with round solid arches, and filled with old barrels. There were Pinsons in Chablis in the time of Napoleon I and probably even before that. Louis Pinson himself took over from his father in 1942 and by 1950 had increased the size of his vineyards from three to five hectares. He is a rare example of a grower in Chablis who has not followed the trend of expansion but has remained content with a small holding, consisting of Les Clos, Forêts, Montmains and Montée de Tonnerre. His methods are traditional: he vinifies in *cuve* and all his wine spends at least six months in old oak barrels. In May 1982 he had not yet bottled his 1980s. As a tasting of 1978 Les Clos showed, he makes wines to keep: the Les Clos was still very youthful and closed, with a firm bite and acidity. The 1973 Les Clos showed the potential towards which the 1978 aspires and beyond, with a richness of flavour, but always the balancing acidity.

Probably Louis Pinson's only claim to innovation is that he was one of the first people in Chablis to own a tractor – in 1958, a year before Moreau!

François Raveneau

François Raveneau has seven hectares of vines that he runs with his son Jean-Marie. They were a combination of his father's and father-in-law's property, together with some purchases of his own. His *grands crus* are Valmur, Les Clos and Blanchot, and his *premiers crus* consist of Montée de Tonnerre, Chapelot, Butteaux, Forêts and Vaillons; he has no simple Chablis. His cellars are the traditional cellars of a small grower, with thick, solid walls and arches and a vaulted ceiling; they are full of *feuillettes* that have an average age of about twenty years.

Raveneau is the essence of tradition in Chablis and for me the essence of quality. His wines have the character that all Chablis should aspire to: a steely austerity, with a long, lingering fruit. His wines are aged in oak for twelve months and are destined to mature in bottle for several more years. In December 1981 Raveneau reckoned that his 1969s were just beginning to drink well. He is also one of two growers in Chablis (the other is René Dauvissat, q.v.) to use wax capsules for his bottles. Initially shy, he has a quiet confidence in his wine and responds to your enthusiasm. Certainly his 1978 Montée de Tonnerre was one of the more memorable wines which I tasted on a visit to Chablis in December

1981. It had great complexity and length, with balancing acidity and fruit, and will not be ready to drink for at least another seven or eight years.

Guy Robin

Guy Robin is an example of a grower who is a little haphazard in his methods, so that the results are sometimes excellent and sometimes disastrous. His estate consists of three hectares of *grands crus* in Blanchot, Valmur and Vaudésir, and nine hectares of *premiers crus* in Butteaux, Vaillons, Mélinots and Montée de Tonnerre. Guy is of the third generation of Robins in Chablis and works with his son Jean-Pierre, who has his own small parcels of Beugnon, Vaillons and Chablis. Mention must also be made of Denise Robin, who is a *femme formidable* in the nicest possible way – a very capable woman, who plays a large part in running the business and organizing her rather scatty husband.

Robin is one of the few growers who still ferment in barrels of 225 litres. It is his *grands crus* that receive this treatment; his other wines are usually fermented in vat, but then spend about six months in old oak.

Domaine Rottiers–Clothilde

Mme Lynne Rottiers was the daughter of a Monsieur Tremblay, a grower at La Chapelle Vaupelteigne, who inherited half of her father's property on his death in 1973. Her Parisian husband helped her to expand their vineyards to some twenty-four hectares, of which ten were not yet in production in July 1981. He then became disenchanted with the narrow horizons of the Chablis hillsides and is now associated with the University of Texas, where he is helping to establish a wine industry, while his wife continues to run the estate. Her *premiers crus* are principally Fourchaume and Montmains and she has five hectares of ordinary Chablis. She bottles her wines young and intends them for relatively early drinking. Her cellars are new and well equipped.

Marcel Servin

Mme Marcel Servin, who is bright and dynamic, has run all the commercial side of the family company since her husband's death. Her son Jean is responsible for the vines and vinification. The family company as such was founded in 1964, but the family's activities as *vignerons* go back much farther than that. They have a particularly close relationship with Alexis Lichine, who describes a visit to them in his book *The Wines of France* (1952). The situation was very different then. Grandpère

Servin was a *tonnelier chez* Monsieur Simmonet across the road, with a few vines of his own, and the business has developed from that small holding into one of fifteen hectares: four of *grands crus* (Les Clos, Blanchot, Preuses and Bougros) and eleven of *premiers crus* (Vaillons, Montée de Tonnerre and Forêts). They installed a new vinification plant in 1981, with temperature-controlled fermentation vats. Eventually they hope to get a refrigeration plant, but at present just leave the wine outside over the winter, which is nearly as effective. Bottling usually takes place a year after the vintage. The company was one of the first to experiment with a mechanical harvester (in 1982).

Philippe Testut

Philippe Testut exudes enthusiasm, charm and talent, and not only does he make excellent Chablis, but he also runs a vineyard in the southern Rhône, in Lirac. It can sometimes be a little difficult trying to be in two places at once: in 1981 the vintage in Chablis started the day after it had finished in Lirac.

Testut began his career in Chablis with Long Depaquit in 1963. His family, whose company manufactures the luggage-weighing machines in all the airports of France, then bought, as newcomers to Chablis, a parcel of Grenouilles in 1966, and the family *domaine* was gradually extended to forty hectares. The family were responsible for the promotion of the name of Château de Grenouilles – in fact, a rather tumbledown farmhouse which is the only building on the *grands crus* slopes where they made their Grenouilles. Following various family problems, almost all of their share of Grenouilles was sold at the end of the 1970s and is now run by a GAEC of growers who also belong to La Chablisienne. It was at this time that Philippe Testut bought his vineyard in Lirac, but he also kept a very small portion of Grenouilles and altogether has seventeen hectares of vines in Chablis, as well as a very small interest in La Moutonne.

Testut uses a mixture of vats and barrels for ageing his wine, depending on the characteristics of the particular vintage. The results show individuality and talent.

Jean Pierre Tricon

A tall, energetic man, Jean Pierre Tricon has a strong sense of purpose and direction and a willingness to air his views. He is a regional delegate for the INAO and sees himself as 'entre les deux clans'. He came to Chablis at the beginning of the 1950s and with his brothers developed a large estate of farmland. He did not plant his first vines until 1968. Now he has twenty-one hectares – mainly of Chablis, with an excellent south-facing aspect, but also some Montmains and Montée de Tonnerre and a small parcel of Bougros, which will come into production in 1984.

Tricon has a new *cuverie*, built in 1979, outside Chablis on the road to Avallon. Everything is spotless, as he is a great exponent of the importance of hygiene in wine-making. His wine is kept mainly in stainless-steel or enamel-lined concrete vats and some of his *premiers crus* also spend three or four months in wood. He envisages using more wood for his *grand cru* when it comes into production. His wine is refrigerated for tartrates and the cellars are temperature-controlled. He bottles under inert gas about a year after the vintage.

Adjoining his modern cellar are the remains of the old cellar, where he keeps a collection of vinous artefacts. Here we tasted a range of his wines that left an impression of good classic Chablis.

All Tricon's wines are sold under the name of Domaine de Vauroux. His label illustrates the distinctive *cabane*: one of the igloo-like shelters, made from large stones, which were built in the vineyards during the eighteenth and nineteenth centuries. Until the 1950s many were still to be seen in the area, but they have now virtually disappeared, with the exception of the one that Tricon has restored in his vineyard. The remains of the *cabanes*, as large clusters of stones, provide interesting evidence of the original extent of the vineyards of Chablis, for they are to be found in places where the woodland is now being cleared for replanting with vines.

Robert Vocoret

Robert Vocoret is a very traditional grower in his methods and attitudes. His grandfather began the family business in 1880, and he himself first began bottling his wines in 1936. The *domaine* now totals some thirty hectares, with Les Clos, Valmur and Blanchot in *grands crus*, an assortment of *premiers crus* (Montée de Tonnerre, Vaillons, Forêts, Montmains, Beugnon, Butteaux, Séchet and Châtains), totalling some thirteen hectares, as well as thirteen hectares of simple Chablis. Both Vocoret and his wife, a rather wizened old lady, still play an active part in a business that their sons will inherit.

Vocoret is one of the few producers who still ferments in large oak barrels or *foudres*. However, despite this, he does not age his wine in wood, for he feels that you would need new barrels every year for it to have any effect and he prefers the uniformity of stainless-steel vats for maturing his wine. Normally he bottles, depending on the malolactic fermentation, a year after the vintage. His cellars are therefore a combination of the old and the new. A 1975 Les Clos, tasted in December 1981, was my 'wine of the week', with complex Chardonnay fruit and an underlying austerity.

Growers in Other Villages

BEINES

Alain Geoffroy
Alain Geoffroy is the Mayor of Beines, one of the areas where there has been the most controversy about the expansion of the vineyards. Certainly Geoffroy supports this expansion; he would call it a revision, not an extension. His grandparents began with two hectares of vines and he now has twenty-five hectares, including some Beauroy and Fourchaume, and some Chablis at Beines and La Chapelle Vaupelteigne.

Geoffroy's techniques follow the methods of classic vinification: a Vaslin press, temperature-controlled fermentation, a *passage au froid* and bottling seven or eight months after the vintage, depending on the evolution of the wine. He aims to make wines with a fresh, fruity character and dislikes the accelerated ageing and loss of freshness that he believes can occur with ageing in oak. His wines are ready for sale within the year; it is up to the customer to mature them.

LA CHAPELLE VAUPELTEIGNE

Adhémar Boudin
Unlike many of the Chablis vineyards, Adhémar Boudin's have not been handed down from generation to generation, but are entirely of his own creation. His father was a *tonnelier* at Fontenay-près-Chablis; however, his mother's family had a few vines, as did his wife's, and these provided the basis for his vineyard. He now has eleven hectares of Petit Chablis, Chablis, Fourchaume and l'Homme Mort, and readily admits that he has benefited from the extension of the appellation. He is now in his sixties and his son is already involved in the business. Their wines are sold under the label of GAEC de Chantemerle. Boudin is an individualist, for he is the only grower to sell l'Homme Mort in bottle; generally it is integrated with Fourchaume. However, the differences between the two wines are only too apparent, as a tasting of the

96

respective 1979s demonstrated. His Petit Chablis refutes all criticism of it as a *vin de primeur*, for it is made from seventy-year-old vines and has a real taste of gunflint.

Boudin exudes enthusiasm; wine-making is certainly one of his passions. Quite simply, 'J'aime ça.' He says his friends find him 'un peu maniaque', for he still follows some of the old traditions, such as filtering 'à la lune', for things apparently go in cycles. The wine is full of life with the new moon, 'comme un petit veau en nouvelle lune' ('like a little calf in the new moon'), and rather turbulent, whereas it dies down in the second half of the moon, so that it is easier to treat then. On the other hand, his *cuverie* is modern, with no wood. You cannot call it a cellar, for it is in the attic, due to the impossibility of building cellars at La Chapelle because of the proximity to the Serein. He also uses a modern centrifuge to clean his must before fermentation, which, he believes, means he has to filter the made wine less. The results are delicious, with plenty of fruit and flavour.

Francis Philippon

Francis Philippon and his brother Jacques are typical growers in that they sell both to the Chablis and Beaune *négoce* and also bottle some of their own wine for private individuals, under the label GAEC de la Fourchaume. They own a total of seventeen hectares of Chablis, Petit Chablis, Fourchaume, Montmains and Vaillons.

Their vinification methods are modern. They age their wine in vat for a year before bottling. If the quality of their wine can be judged from a 1980 Fourchaume (long, with good acidity in May 1982), which won a gold medal at the Paris Agricultural Fair, it seems a pity that most of their production disappears into a *négociant*'s mélange.

Jacques Tremblay

Jacques Tremblay is a very typical small grower. His grandfather was a *vigneron* in the 1880s; he himself took over from his father in 1950 and up to 1968 sold all his wine in bulk to *négociants* in Beaune. He then began to bottle a little, but in difficult and uncertain years (like 1978 or 1980) he falls back entirely on the *négoce*.

His vineyards total seven hectares, including two separate hectares of Fourchaume, one near La Chapelle Vaupelteigne and the other close to Preuses. They are apparently very different in the style of wine they produce. Tremblay makes his Chablis as simply as possible, aims for a natural precipitation of the tartrates and bottles in March with a mobile bottling machine, like many small growers. There is no wood to be seen in his cellar: 'J'en suis ennemi,' he says. He prefers the taste of young wine.

CHICHÉE

Luc Michaut
Luc Michaut is almost better known for Epineuil than for Chablis, for he is involved in his son's projects for the renovation of the old vineyards of Epineuil. Apart from a small parcel of Epineuil, he has a hectare of Vaucoupin and five hectares of Chablis near Chichée. His methods are traditional: he bottles eighteen months after the vintage and his wines are aged partly in vat and partly in barrel. He does nothing about tartrates, but allows them to fall naturally. 'Je n'ai pas besoin de massacrer mon vin.'

Nearly all his wine is sold to private individuals from all over the world, including a Japanese who calls in person to collect his wine regularly every year. Michaut's house at Chichée dates back to 1685, but the cellars underneath are even older – sixteenth- and early seventeenth-century – and contain a collection of old agricultural implements and other vinous curiosities.

COURGIS

Gilbert Race
Gilbert Race is the Mayor of Courgis. He is a solid *costeau* type, a farmer as much as a *vigneron*, for he began with cows and grazing land as well as vines. Like most of the growers in Courgis, he belongs to La Chablisienne, but he also makes wine for his daughter, who owns small parcels of Montmains and Chablis, and so fortunately his wines can also be found under her name of Françoise Mougin Race. His wines are kept in vat and old oak barrels and are bottled between twelve and eighteen months after the vintage.

He has a rather attractive old cellar, containing a collection of bottles, full and empty, from all over the world, from Scotch Whisky to Chinese wine. His cellars also house one of the old public wine presses of Courgis; it dates back 150 years.

FLEYS

André Philippon
The pretty village of Fleys is on the road to Tonnerre. Unlike many of the growers in the village, André Philippon is not a member of the

co-operative, but bottles as much as 70 per cent of his wine; the rest goes to the *négoce*. He reproaches his fellow-growers for their lack of dynamism – a quality in which he is certainly not lacking himself. He deals mainly with private individuals, and has had no difficulty in selling his wine, despite the recent fluctuations on the market.

His property consists of seven hectares: five in Mont de Milieu and two in Chablis. His father and grandfather were *vignerons* before him and presumably his six-month-old son will follow in his father's footsteps.

His *cuverie* was recently modernized by the installation of new stainless steel vats. His wines spend two to three months in oak, but he is essentially aiming to make wine with the fruity taste of the grape, rather than with the old-fashioned taste of oak and tannin. The tartrates are left to fall naturally and he expects his wines to mature for five to ten years.

Rather surprisingly, Philippon is an enthusiastic claret-drinker, with excellent taste; Pétrus and Haut Brion are particular favourites.

FONTENAY-PRÈS-CHABLIS

Guy Mothe

Guy Mothe has built up his thirteen hectares of vines himself by buying land that was available for planting. He now has parcels of Fourchaume, Bougros, Vaucoupin and Petit Chablis, and seven hectares of Chablis.

Eighty per cent of Mothe's wine is sold to the Beaune *négoce*. The wine he keeps spends six months in vat before bottling by a mobile bottling machine from Beaune. If the quality of his wine is to be judged by an anonymous half-bottle (he thought it was 1975 Fourchaume, but it had never been labelled!) it is a pity he sells so much to the *négoce*, for it had a lovely, nutty Chardonnay nose, very elegant, with plenty of fruit and a long finish. His 1980 Chablis was good, too.

LIGNORELLES

Gérard Vandevielle

Gérard Vandevielle has a small holding of six hectares at Lignorelles, a village in the northern part of the Chablisien that has been at the centre of some of the controversy over the extension of the appellation. The soil at Lignorelles is mainly portlandian, with very little kimmeridgian, and the village is known mainly for its Petit Chablis. However, in common with other growers in the village, Vandevielle does not approve of the name Petit Chablis. It sounds inferior, he thinks.

The name Vandevielle sounds more Belgian than French. In fact, he is not sure about his origins, as his father was abandoned as a baby and never knew his parents. Gérard Vandevielle inherited a few vines from his father and has developed his vineyard from those.

His six hectares of vines are divided equally between Chablis and Petit Chablis. He bottles some Chablis himself for sale to private customers; the rest goes to the *négoce*. Most of the growers in Lignorelles are members of the co-operative and there is no one with more than twenty hectares of vines.

Vandevielle's cellar is quite modern, with enamel-lined vats and not an oak barrel in sight. His 1978 Chablis was drinking very well in September 1982.

LIGNY-LE-CHÂTEL

Domaine Froment-Moindrot
Although the cellars of M. and Mme Froment are at Ligny-le-Châtel on the northern edge of the Chablisien, their vines are at Poinchy, at its centre. They own three hectares of Beauroy (which they proudly consider to be the best part of Beauroy, as, since it was planted, the appellation has been considerably extended at the expense of the Bois de Beauroy) and, rather curiously, a hectare of Pinot Noir, also at Poinchy, which only merits the appellation of Bourgogne Rouge. A vineyard of Chardonnay would be more profitable, but they wanted to be able to supply their customers with red as well as white wine. Mme Froment did admit that the other growers 'nous ont ri au nez'.

Their small cellars contain a mixture of enamel-lined vats and oak barrels, and their Chablis is aged for about eighteen months before bottling. Surprisingly, their red wine receives less ageing, but this is for reasons of expediency, as they do not have enough stock to meet the demand.

MALIGNY

Lamblin et Fils
Unlike the other Chablis *négociants*, the house of Lamblin is based at Maligny, to the north of Chablis. It is a family firm; the grandfather of the present head of the company was a *viticulteur* and in 1950 his son expanded his activities as a *courtier* to those of a négociant. Today the company is run by Jacques Lamblin, whose son and daughter-in-law are also involved in the business.

Their vineyards consist of Les Clos and Valmur in *grands crus*, Fourchaume and Mont de Milieu in *premiers crus* and some Chablis and Petit Chablis around Maligny. However, their *négociant* activities embrace a wider range of Chablis and on the home market they also deal in wines from the Côte d'Or. In addition, 15 per cent of their turnover comes from a table wine (a Blanc de Blancs), and bulk sales form an important part of their business. Their *sous marques* include Jacques Arnouls, Jacques de la Ferté, Paul Jarry and Bernard Mille.

Their premises are new and very modern: temperature-controlled installations, stainless-steel vats, refrigeration units and filter machines. Somehow it is all too modern, for although their wines are young and fresh, they seem to lack any depth or flavour.

Jean Durup

There have been Durups at Maligny since the fifteenth century. Jean Durup's great-grandfather tended the vines of the Château de Maligny for thirty years at the end of the last century and it is part of that vineyard that Jean Durup has replanted. He is now also the owner of the ruined Château de Maligny, which he is gradually restoring to its former splendour, with moat and cellars. Some of his wine is sold under the name of Château de Maligny, and his other labels are

The Château de Maligny, which dates back to the twelfth century, has had a chequered history. It is now being restored by Jean Durup

Jean Durup, president of the Fédération des Viticulteurs Chablisiens and owner of Domaine de l'Eglantière at Maligny

Domaine de l'Eglantière, Domaine de Paulière and Domaine de Valéry. His seventy-three-hectare estate is largely a recent creation, made possible by the extension of the appellation. Jean Durup was one of those tempted by the renewed profitability of the vineyards to return to Chablis and revive his interest in his family's property. His estate now includes eleven hectares of Fourchaume and a sizeable parcel of new plantings in the *premiers crus* and simple Chablis, but no *grands crus*. Durup is a fine figure of a man, of solid stature, with a magnificent beard. He spends his week-days in Paris, running a successful tax advisory company; in his absence his estate is ably managed by his *chef de cave*, the likeable and very hospitable Michel Poitout. Oak has been banished from the spotless, tiled Durup cellars; the wine is kept in cement vats lined with fibreglass and, apart from refrigerating for tartrates, it is given the minimum amount of treatment. The results are successful: fruity, almost flowery Chablis, with some character but not a great deal of weight. In May 1981 a simple 1973 Chablis was showing very well, and a 1978 Fourchaume had a rich honey and vegetable nose, with a similarly complex palate and a crisp bite on the finish. The 1973 ratafia, drunk with a *duché* biscuit, is also to be highly recommended.

Roger Séguinot

Roger Séguinot and his son Daniel have between them about twelve hectares of Fourchaume, Chablis and Petit Chablis. The family have been at Maligny for several generations. His great grandfather served under Napoleon III and was described as a *viticulteur* in his *livret militaire*.

For Roger Séguinot an oak barrel no longer gives anything to a wine; he uses cement vats for storage and bottles about fourteen months after the vintage. He believes that Petit Chablis is not merely a *vin de primeur*, but, after tasting his 1979, I must confess that I was not convinced. Although I found his wines a little characterless, Séguinot himself makes up for any deficiencies in them. He is a firm believer in the expansion of the vineyards and airs his views with a lively enthusiasm.

MILLY

Bernard Barat

Bernard Barat arrived in Chablis in 1947, when he married a *vigneron*'s daughter and began working with his father-in-law. There were no tractors then; they each had a horse and grazing land for the horses. He now has just two hectares of vines in Vaillons, Côte de Léchet and Chablis; the other three hectares that made up his exploitation have been passed on to his son, who is building up his own vineyards.

Barat is a small man, with twinkling blue eyes, who was happy to discuss Chablis past and present over a glass of his 1980 Vaillons, which is the only wine he bottles himself. It accounts for a fifth of his production; the rest is sold equally between the *négoces* of Beaune and Chablis. Barat has a philosophical attitude to the changes he has seen: 'On faisait du vin comme papa autrefois, sans trop chercher à comprendre.' Now phenomena like the malolactic fermentation are better understood, but we still have much to learn. New processes are tried out, but 'on revient toujours aux mêmes principes'.

He ferments in both vat and barrel, but prefers a fermentation in vat as it is more uniform and easier to control in a larger volume. His wine is usually left in vat on its lees until midsummer, and then fined before being bottled by a mobile bottling machine from Mâcon.

POINCHY

Madeleine Coquard

Madeleine Coquard is nearly eighty. She lives alone in a large house in Poinchy with her cats and dogs and chickens. She is a small grey-haired old lady, with bright eyes. 'Je ne vais pas pouvoir vous raconter grande chose,' she said, but remembers Chablis in the 1920s, when the life of a *vigneron* was hard. Her family have been farmers and *viticulteurs* at Poinchy for at least two hundred years, and she followed in the family footsteps because there was nothing else for her to do; as she says, she was not educated to do anything else. At first, she did not like it, but now she does. Sadly, however, she is the last of her family and there will be no one to take over her couple of hectares of Chablis and Côte de Léchet.

Her methods are somewhat rustic; she has an old cellar under her house, dating back to 1840, and a mixture of old *feuillettes* and some cement vats. Until the early 1960s she sold all her wine to the *négoce*; now she bottles a little, mainly for private customers. Her wines all seem to have a hard bite to them, wines to which the quotation might apply, 'J'aime ce Chablis, c'est si dur, presque brutal.'

Gérard Tremblay

A young grower who inherited twelve hectares from his father, Gérard Tremblay (no relation of Bernard or Jacques Tremblay) has been gradually increasing his *domaine* since 1975, so that he now has thirty hectares of vines. They are made up of four hectares of Petit Chablis, sixteen of Chablis (including a new planting of nine hectares at Beines, that was funded by the SAFER) and, in *premiers crus*, Fourchaume (5.5 hectares), Montmains (1.5 hectares) and Côte de Léchet (three hectares). His installations are new and modern, with stainless-steel vats and a system of temperature control for the fermentation. It was, therefore, rather a surprise to find a cellar containing small *foudres* and also a few new oak *fûts*. Tremblay is experimenting with the effects of ageing his wine in new oak for six months, and we tasted his 1979 Chablis, which had received this treatment. There was a strong bouquet of new oak, which faded in the air; the flavour was fuller and more rounded than traditional Chablis, with an unmistakable underlying oakiness. More often his wines are aged in vat for six months.

Although he has a more broad-minded attitude to new ideas than the average Chablis growers, Tremblay is moderate in his innovations. His enthusiasm for what he is doing is evident and he is anxious to promote his wines, which are sold under the label Domaine des Iles, mainly on the export market.

PRÉHY

Bernard Légland

Bernard Légland bears a striking resemblance to the film star Jack Nicholson. He is an example of a young grower who has developed his own vineyard. He began in 1976 by renting a few vines and has grown from this small beginning, so that he now has 2.5 hectares of Montmains, with another 1.5 hectares to plant and five hectares of Chablis.

All Légland's wine is sold in bottle under the name of Domaine des Maronniers. As yet none is exported, as he is concentrating his efforts on the home market in an attempt to get Chablis better known in France. His horizons extend far beyond the typical 'mentalité du petit pays', and he has the energetic attitude of someone with a sense of purpose and a belief in his objectives. None of his wine goes into wood; the few *feuillettes* in his cellar are there for visual effect. His wine is refrigerated and bottled young. I found his Chablis very perfumed and flowery, almost Alsace in character, which he said was typical of the terrain. For me it was an attractive wine, but not typical Chablis.

VILLY

Julien Baillard

Julien Baillard is a character. He has a rich, fruity Burgundian accent and enjoys talking about his wines to a receptive audience. He is reaching retirement age, and his five hectares of Chablis and Fourchaume and a little Petit Chablis will go to his son-in-law Jean Servin, and through another daughter to his grandson Matthieu. He ferments his wine in both barrel and in vat, but believes that fermentation in wood gives the wine more character. The ends of his barrels are painted bright yellow, which looked rather attractive in his small arched cellar. In the corner were potatoes and pots of jam. It was all rather rustic, with chickens being plucked in the yard in preparation for the invasion of *vendangeurs* the following week.

Julian Baillard aims to make wines that will mature slowly in bottle. A 1966 simple Chablis was still amazingly youthful, with light Chardonnay fruit.

Other Growers, listed by Location

CHABLIS
Felix Besson
Maurice Michel
Christian Mignard
Roger Moreau

BEINES
R. Franchet
Jean-Claude Gaumont
Sylvain Mosnier
Robert Naulin
Daniel Roblot

BERU
Henri Bocquet

LA CHAPELLE VAUPELTEIGNE
Domaine Pascal Bouchard
Bernard Tremblay

CHEMILLY-SUR-SEREIN
Jean-Pierre and Joel Vilain
(Domaine de Guet-Soleil)

CHICHÉE
Roland Jacquinot
Lucien Merschiltz et Fils
GAEC Molusson Frères

COURGIS
Donatien Landais
Bernard Race
Jean Race

FLEYS
Jean and Alain Gautheron
Michel and Jean-Pierre Grossot
Roger and Claude Laroche
Paul and Robert Nicole

FONTENAY-PRÈS-CHABLIS
Lucien de Oliveira
Raymond Roy

LIGNORELLES
Michel Boudin
Marc and Pierre Hamelin
Raymond Laventurieux
Georges Massé
Alain Pautré
René Rey
Maurice Sourice

MALIGNY
Robert Jolly
Pierre Lasnier
Maurice Vocoret

MILLY
Bernard Defaix
Jean Defaix
Pierre des Courtis
Jean-Jack and Robert Fourrey
Henri Coulaudin

POINCHY
Claude Châtelain
Gulbeng Magarian
Jacques Morin

PRÉHY
Christian Adine
Gaston Sauvageau
Philippe Séguin

VILLY
Maurice Dupignet

6
THE 'OTHER CHABLIS' AND OTHER PROBLEMS

Chablis is the best known white wine in the world – or, more accurately, the best known white wine name. For in so many parts of the world it has come to be a generic term for a dry, light, fruity white wine, often of no specific origins. A selection of wine lists from Trinidad, for example, produced Mountain Chablis, Chablis Nature, Gold Chablis, Ruby Chablis, Pink Chablis – none of them French and some of them not even white. The Liquor Control Board of Alberta, Canada, even lists 'London Chablis' – that is, Chablis from London, Ontario!

There is nothing new in this abuse of the name of Chablis. Before the days of *appellation contrôlée* the production of over eighty villages in the Yonne went under its all-encompassing name. The confusion of terminology was by no means confined to France, nor is it a recent development.

Imitations

In his *Report on Cheap Wines* (published in 1865, after Gladstone had lowered the duty on French wine), Dr Druitt refers to Hungarian Chablis, obtainable from Denmans at 16s a bottle, which he noted as 'a light wine, of light straw colour, not too acid, rather too much bouquet'. He also mentions finding cheap Chablis at 18s ('a thin light clean wine, appetizing and of pleasant flavour') and capital Chablis at 24s and 30s a bottle. Dr Druitt, who was a member of the College of Physicians, valued wine as a tonic: 'I often used to prescribe a cheap Chablis at about 1s 6d a bottle, sold by E. Brun of 63 Dean Street, Soho and found even poor dispensary patients satisfied with it.' I do not think one dare enquire too closely into the provenance of this particular cheap Chablis.

Only a few years later, in 1877, Charles Tovey comments on the abuse of the name Chablis.[1] After extolling the virtues of Chablis, he says, 'so much white wine is sold in France, as well as in other

---

[1] *Wine and Wine Countries.*

countries, especially England, that is not Chablis at all, that the wine gets an ill-reputation which it does not deserve. I have known petit Graves labelled and sold as Chablis and I question if the real produce of Chablis is to be had at any hotel or restaurant.'

André Simon relates[1] how, as a young man who had just joined the wine trade in the early 1900s, he shared a bottle of 1893 Corton Charlemagne, from Louis Latour, with a rather more senior member of the trade. The conversation went something like this:

> *'Well, young fellow, my lad, how do you like this Chablis?'*
> *'You mean Corton, sir?'*
> *'Tut, tut,' snorted the old gentleman, 'don't try and be so clever and don't fuss us with all manner of French names. You had better remember that in this country all white Burgundies are called Chablis.'*

As an experienced member of the wine trade, André Simon (in his textbook for the trade, published in 1920[2]) exhorts his colleagues not to perpetrate the continuation of fake Chablis: 'Genuine Chablis is never cheap, because there is so little of it; faked Chablis is always dear and yet there is a lot of it. If your customers will not pay the price of genuine Chablis, offer them some other white wine, under some other name, but never under the name of Chablis, not even if you have it in Burgundy bottles, not even if you have a stock of Chablis labels, not even if you qualify the name "Chablis" by some other geographical appellation.'

It would seem that his words did not have much effect, for one can cite a reference (1934) by Stephen Gwynn[3] to a London club, 'whose wine committee should have known better', that served a wine labelled Chablis Meursault. Gwynn also writes that 'it is agreed on all hands that no name in all the commerce of wine is more abused than Chablis. Anything less like the wine which is made there than what is often sold by that name in England would be difficult to imagine.' And, writing a few years earlier, Warner Allen mentions 'the humble muscadet masquerading behind a chablis label'.[4]

To quote André Simon again: 'Few wines have suffered to the same extent as Chablis from that most objectionable form of flattery which is

---

[1] *Vintagewise.*
[2] *The Blood of the Grape.*
[3] *Burgundy.*
[4] *The Romance of Wine.*

called imitation.'[1] The abuse of the name is an indication of the popularity and success of the wine and the consequence of a lack of regulations defining the place of origin. Great Britain was not obliged to conform to the *appellation contrôlée* regulations until it joined the Common Market in 1973. Until then it was perfectly legitimate for an English wine merchant to buy the excess stock of a Chablis producer – that is, the wine not entitled to *appellation contrôlée* status – and sell it as Chablis.

Similarly, it was perfectly acceptable (in law), and very common, to find the dry white table wines of Spain labelled as Spanish Chablis, in the same way that the sweet white wine of the country was called Spanish Sauternes and much of the red wine Spanish Burgundy. It was only the Champagne shippers who had succeeded in protecting their name against this kind of abuse (but only in Europe) when they won a court case in 1958 against the Costa Brava Wine Company, who were selling a sparkling wine from Perellada as Spanish Champagne. From 1973, however, so-called Spanish Chablis could only be sold as Spanish dry white wine.

If the name Chablis is now protected throughout Europe, under the auspices of the Common Market, the problem still survives outside Europe – particularly in California. So-called Californian Chablis was found in London as early as 1906. It doubtless disappeared during the years of Prohibition, but then returned to the American market, and in subsequent years has been sold in ever-increasing quantities, as more and more Americans have turned to dry white wines, deserting their traditional cocktails. The caption of the Daumier print (p. 111) illustrates the situation perfectly. To many Americans Chablis means a dry white wine of Californian origin, what they call a 'jug wine'. The European equivalent is a table wine, a *vin de table*, without any indication of precise origins. In his recent book[2] Professor Maynard Amerine quotes the American Wine Institute's recommendations (1978) that Californian Chablis be 'light medium straw in colour, light to medium in body, of medium acidity, fruity, well-balanced and have a good bottle bouquet' – in other words, a very ordinary wine of no particular character. However I could not help being amused by Amerine's footnote to the Wine Institute's definition: 'Very wishful thinking'.

Most Californian Chablis is made from a blend of grapes. The prolific table grape that is also used for wine, Thompson Seedless, is

[1] Op. cit.
[2] *The Technology of Winemaking.*

usually the dominant grape variety, or varietal, among Chenin Blanc, Folle Blanche, Green Hungarian, Pinot Blanc and so on. Usually they are grown in the Central Valley of California, where irrigated vineyards produced grapes in prolific quantities. The large wineries (like Gallo, Italian Swiss Colony, Paul Masson and Almadén) are particularly responsible for the production of Californian Chablis, and it is in connection with Gallo that the INAO fought a court case in Bermuda in 1982 to protect the name of Chablis.

The case was based on English law, for Bermuda is still a British colony, subject to English common law and English legislation. Consequently, Bermuda should conform to the acceptance of the French laws of *appellation contrôlée*, as they stand in Britain. So thought the INAO, who brought an injunction against J. E. Lightbourne, the importers of Gallo wines, to prevent them from using the word Chablis to describe their Californian white table wine. The court's ruling, given in July 1982, was that the term Chablis could no longer be used in Bermuda after 30 November that year. This decision was of enormous significance for the protection of the name Chablis, as well as of such other abused names as Burgundy and Champagne. It is expected that the rest of the Caribbean countries will conform to the ruling and that the effects will also be felt in the United States, for Bermuda is one of the favourite holiday resorts of many Americans and the marketing of Californian wines in Bermuda will have to be adjusted accordingly.

Australia is also guilty of abuse of the name of Chablis, commonly used there to describe a dry white wine of no particular origins, usually made from Ugni Blanc and Sémillon grapes. Perhaps because Australia is not such a significant market for genuine Chablis as is the United States, the effects of the Australian purloining of the name are less serious.

The latest comer to the range of imitation Chablis is Mexican Chablis. The new wine industry of what was once called Baja, or Lower California, is presumably imitating its northern neighbours.

The abuse of the name Chablis has not been confined to still wine, but has also extended to sparkling wine. The origins of the company of Simmonet-Febvre (see Chapter 5, 'La Chablisienne and Négociants in Chablis') stem from the production of sparkling wine. Perhaps it was their Sparkling Chablis that was referred to in the 1906 edition of Mrs Beeton's *Household Management*. The suitability of the dry white wines of the Yonne for conversion into sparkling wine was recognized in Champagne, and certainly before the introduction of the laws of *appellation controlée* a considerable amount of Chablis found its way to Reims and Epernay. Writing in the 1930s, C. W. Berry[1] mentions dining in Auxerre over 'a small bottle of sparkling Chablis which was atrocious' and over one of Auxerre Rosé ('the least said of this the soonest mended'). Today the house of Simmonet-Febvre continue to make sparkling wine, which is sold as Bourgogne Mousseux. Paul Masson markets Crackling Chablis in the United States and even Her Majesty's Customs and Excise say that 'Chablis may be either sparkling or still, depending on manufacture'![2] Whatever gave them that idea?

Old Californian grower to another,
in the Golden Nugget Tavern,
Napa Valley:
'D'you know what I just
heard! . . . Chablis wine,
they make it in
France too!'

This cartoon (with thanks to Daumier for the picture) wittily illustrates the problems caused by the use and abuse of the name 'Chablis' in other parts of the world

The Commercial Situation of Chablis today

One of the causes of the abuse of the name Chablis has been the shortage of authentic Chablis. The area of production is tiny, compared with that of many other wines, and much of the land entitled to the appellation remained unplanted, especially in the years following the Second World War, before the development of effective frost protec-

[1] *In Search of Wine.*
[2] Notice 15.

tion methods assured the growers of a viable living. The annual production of Chablis was miniscule, compared to the demand for it on the world market. Yields were much lower, as the vineyards were less healthy. In the 1950s the five hundred or so hectares of vines produced an average yield of about twenty-five hectolitres per hectare. Today yields are much higher, with healthier vines and more effective frost protection, and, with the incentive of a more secure livelihood for the growers and their workers, the area of the vineyards has increased enormously. Of the 5,250 hectares that are eligible for *appellation contrôlée* status, 1,667 were planted in 1982, although the most dramatic period of growth came in the 1970s, as Appendix 5 shows.

New vineyards cannot be planted, nor old ones revived, without money, and, in the case of Chablis, the support of the Crédit Agricole. This bank was originally set up by farmers for farmers and, in rural communities where farmland and vineyards abound, is an important element in the agricultural economy. The Crédit Agricole in Chablis estimates that it has financed ninety-five per cent of the extensions to the vineyards of Chablis. Its policy favours young growers: those who are planting new vines will not have to begin repaying their loan until their vines have begun to produce wine, four years after the commencement of the loan. Help is also given to those who need to obtain equipment and machinery, particularly the expensive installations required to combat frost, and the Crédit Agricole also helps the growers during bad times. A large sum of money was lent to growers in 1980, when few of them were able to sell much of the 1979 vintage. Despite the severe price fluctuations and market swings of recent years, most growers make a successful living out of their vines, and there is greater affluence in Chablis than there was twenty, and certainly thirty, years ago.

As we have seen, the increase in the area of the vineyards of Chablis has not been accomplished without controversy; the arguments for and against it, in relation to the quality of Chablis, have been discussed in the context of the activities of the INAO (see p. 45). What concerns us here is the current commercial situation of Chablis. Is the world market able to absorb the large increase in the supply of genuine Chablis, and at the same rate? Is there a need to regulate the supply of Chablis, and thereby its price?

Chablis is an agricultural product and, like all agricultural products, subject to the weather for its success or failure. Situated as the vineyards are, on the northern edge of the wine-producing belt of Europe, they are more affected by climatic conditions than most. We only need to look at the yields of the last decade (Appendix 3) to see the enormous fluctuations in production that occurred. During ten years the average annual yield fluctuated between 27 and 77 hectolitres per hectare, and the total production varied from 43,022 hectolitres in 1981 to over three times as much (114,227 hectolitres) in 1979.

During the 1960s the situation had been no better. As Peter Sichel very aptly says in his vintage report of November 1968, the problem in Chablis is, in fact, not one of making wines of quality, but of making wine at all.[1]

It is the simple law of supply and demand that affects the price. In his January 1970 vintage report Peter Sichel surveys the prices of the 1960s. Taking the vineyard price of Chablis as 100 in 1958, he shows the evolution of the prices as follows:

1958	100	1964	93
1959	136	1965	90
1960	144	1966	90
1961	162	1967	118
1962	114	1968	114
1963	72	1969	214

In 1956 there were severe frosts, a shortage developed, and five years later, with the small crop of 1961, prices reached a peak. The growers then lost a large part of their traditional market to Mâcon, Muscadet and Pouilly Fuissé, as the competitors of basic Chablis. The demand fell and so did prices. For seven years prices remained reasonable and customers were slowly won back. Then, between 1967 and 1969, there were two small crops and the third was of poor quality, so that prices escalated again. With 1970 came a hitherto record crop of 74,498 hectolitres, well over three times the production of 1969, which helped to remedy the shortage of Chablis on the market.

The year 1970 saw the establishment in Chablis of a committee, or Commission, of growers and *négociants*, formed in an attempt to stabilize prices and prevent such wild fluctuations. Although with the small 1971 vintage there was a 40 per cent increase on the price of the 1970 vintage, which may have made the Commission's efforts seem

[1] The annual vintage reports written by Peter Allen Sichel (of Maison Sichel, in Bordeaux) provide a fascinating survey of the rise and fall of the Chablis market over the last twenty years.

ineffectual, in fact it did prevent another excessive price explosion.

This Commission, consisting of the growers and principal buyers – namely, the *négociants* of Chablis, Beaune and Bordeaux – as well as Nicolas in Paris, maintained prices in the face of considerable difficulties for about four years. In 1972 the growers resisted offers exceeding a ten per cent increase on the prices of 1971, and 1973 continued in stability, when elsewhere in France prices were rising. The discipline of the Commission began to disintegrate when prices fell with the recession of 1974; disagreements among its members occurred and it was disbanded. In 1976 the protective insularity of Chablis was ruptured and prices doubled in six months, with high offers from buyers seeking to replace their unfilled requirements of Côte d'Or and Mâconnais wines. Peter Sichel was not exaggerating when he began his 1978 vintage report with the words, 'Chablis seems to have gone mad.' With the 1977 vintage prices had escalated still further, for a vintage whose quality did not warrant the increase. Ill-founded optimism and euphoria seemed to prevail, a climate perhaps similar to that of Bordeaux in 1972. Growers in Chablis were offered 3,500 francs per *feuillette* for the 1978 vintage, as opposed to 2,200 francs for the 1977 vintage, by *négociants* in Beaune who were anxious to secure their requirements in a situation of insufficient supply. But demand was not equal to the excessive prices. To quote Peter Sichel again,[1] 'As one grower rather gruesomely put it "A fall in price is as inevitable as death. As with death, the only question is when." ' And sure enough, the crash came – with the large 1979 vintage.

Many members of the traditional clientèle of Chablis, the fine wine merchants and restaurants of Britain and the United States, resisted these increases and looked elsewhere for white wine. The opening prices of the 1979s were 40 per cent below the average prices of the 1978s and the price of the 1980 vintage fell still further. As one *négociant* said in retrospect, it is hard to overestimate the damage done by the excessive prices of the 1978s. The table, which gives the ex-cellar prices of a bottle of Chablis from 1970 until 1982,[2] shows just how much the prices have fluctuated over this period. A small vintage in 1981 did something to redress the situation, but 1982 produced a record-breaking 116,897 hectolitres. After a hardening of the prices for the 1981 vintage, prices fell again with this large crop – a fall which fortunately coincided

[1] Report on the vintage of 1978.
[2] The figures were provided by a *négociant* in Chablis.

with renewed interest in Chablis, on the export markets, especially from America, in view of the favourable exchange rate. As the grapes of the abundant 1983 vintage were being picked, little of the 1982 vintage remained in the cellars of Chablis.

Prices of Chablis ex-cellar per bottle in francs

1970	7	1977	20
1971	8	1978	29
1972	9	1979	19
1973	9	1980	16
1974	7.50	1981	24
1975	8.50	1982	18
1976	12		

Essentially, high and low prices come in waves. They are affected to a certain extent by quality, but infinitely more important are the size of the last vintage and (in the period between April and the harvest) the expected production of the next vintage, combined with the demand over the previous six months and the expectation of future demand. The buyer's psychology is one of an expectation of falling prices. As Martin Forde explains,[1] there are phases when there is a psychology of glut and phases when there is a pyschology of penury: 'What has been acutely embarrassing about Chablis is that there is always either too much of it or not enough, and that the glut or shortage is extremely important.' When prices are low, buyers tend to over-cover their needs, anticipating rising prices and a possible shortage with the next vintage, and often negotiate volume discounts. Prices only start to rise when the buyers are certain that they can fall no further, and they increase until the buyers begin reducing their purchases with the fear of customer resistance to high prices. Sales slow down, with buyers either covering their minimum needs or not buying at all; then the prices start to fall and the demand dries up until they can fall no further.

Another significant factor is the speed with which information is now circulated, particularly since the advent of the telex, so that major buyers in the United States know about a disastrous frost or hail-storm within hours of it happening and can react to the situation accordingly.

The policy of expansion in the Chablis vineyards was designed in part to alleviate the supply situation and to prevent the violent price

[1] 'Chablis: The Law of the Market'.

fluctuations mentioned above. But the situation did not improve during the 1970s and, in fact, was probably worse then than during the 1960s, before the programme of planting had really begun. However, growers like Mme Coquard (who remember the 1920s and 1930s) will tell you that it was no better then. The world-wide economic crisis of the early 1930s, combined with the shortage of wine from small vintages, caused enormous price fluctuations. William Fèvre has traced the price fluctuations of Chablis from 1920 to 1981, and the resulting graph is a dramatic illustration of the frightening rise and fall of the price of the *feuillette* in successive, never-ending waves (see Appendix 8).

There may, therefore, be an argument for regulating the amount of wine allowed on to the market by the instigation of a system of *bloquage*. There is an element among the growers and *négociants* that favours a system of stock control, or *bloquage*, that would limit the quantity of wine that they would be allowed to sell to fifty hectolitres per hectare each year. This would provide a safeguard against excessive price rises at times of small vintages and control the stock situation at times of large vintages. A buffer stock could thus be created that would maintain a stability and continuity of supply, so that the market would be neither flooded nor depleted.

However, others see this idea merely as beautiful theory that would be impractical to implement. As I have said earlier, many of the growers sell must direct to the *négociants*, and, in some cases, have no storage facilities for wine, let alone facilities for making it. Consequently, some *négociants* fear that a system of *bloquage* would lead to a deterioration in quality, if ill-equipped growers have to store their own wine and the system throws all the responsibility and expense of storage onto the *négociants*. Furthermore, Chablis consists of numerous different *crus*, apart from simple Chablis, and this would cause further complications. There are also doubts about the efficient operation of the machinery of *bloquage*, in that it may be too slow to react to a given situation. However, it is a system that is already used in Alsace and Muscadet, and regulatory stock measures are also in operation for Côtes du Rhône and in the Mâconnais.

Although Chablis would undoubtedly benefit from a regulatory system of stable prices, and a continuity of supply, as was achieved to some extent in the early 1970s, there is a general reluctance to accept the idea. In fact, at a meeting in June 1980 some measure of agreement over a system of bloquage was achieved, but personalities and conflicting interests came into play and the agreement was short-lived, so that no effective action was taken. After the enormous 1982 vintage there are again signs of a willingness to attempt to organize the market and of an acceptance of the need to control stocks and prices. A meeting of the *syndicats* at the beginning of November 1982 reached some measure of agreement. The *syndicats* may have been spurred on by the threat of interference by the recently created Office du Vin, preferring to organize themselves rather than let the Government do it for them. As yet, it is too early to see the effects of their discussions.

Any system of *bloquage* would need a responsible body, such as an independent Comité Interprofessionnel, to organize and administer it. At present Chablis is grouped with the Comité Interprofessionnel of the Côte d'Or, based nearly a hundred miles away, in Beaune. When the CIB was set up in 1966, this was a logical arrangement, since a very large part of the production of Chablis was bought by the Beaune *négoce*, who were the first buyers to distribute Chablis on any scale, at a time when most of the growers of Chablis were content merely to provide the *négociants* with wine. In recent years, however, an increasing number of growers have begun to bottle and sell an increasing proportion of their wine under their own label, rather than sell must to the *négociants*. Yet, despite this movement towards independence, there is still a certain amount of apathy towards the idea of a Comité Interprofessionnel. Although the vineyard area of Chablis has grown so much over the last decade, many people still think Chablis is too small to have its own Comité Interprofessionnel and many people's thinking is still orientated towards Beaune. It would necessitate a decree from the Ministry of Agriculture to set up a separate Comité Interprofessionnel, and numerous bureaucratic complications could well be entailed. One grower referred to the idea as 'la rigolade' ('a farce'); another considered it merely a panacea to be applied when times are hard. However, others believe that only a Comité Interprofessionnel could provide the structure and stability that the region so badly needs.

The Reputation of Chablis and the Export Market

Chablis rivals Champagne as the most exported and the best-known French wine. About 80 per cent of the total production of Chablis is drunk outside France, but, unlike Champagne, which the French appreciate with enthusiasm, Chablis is hardly known in France. Otherwise well-informed people enquire whether Chablis is red or white: they are not quite sure where the place is, and, when they remember, exclaim, 'Oh yes, my grandfather used to drink it!' Writing in 1962, Françoise Grivot says, 'The mass of ordinary restaurants in France have forgotten about Chablis, even in the immediate area.'[1] This can be supported by a story told by Michel Rémon that illustrates not only the general ignorance of the French about Chablis, but also their regional chauvinism when confronted with wines from any area other than their own. At some time in the 1950s his father was dining in one of Bordeaux's finer restaurants, that shall remain nameless. He had ordered alose, the local fish speciality, and to a Chablisien it seemed natural to accompany it with a bottle of Chablis. However, not only was there no Chablis on the wine list, but the wine waiter exclaimed, 'Mais Monsieur, vous n'allez pas boire des saloperies comme ça!' ('You aren't going to drink that sort of rubbish!'). So that was how Chablis was regarded in a wine region on the other side of France. Even in Auxerre, the nearest town of any size to Chablis, and only fifteen miles away, it is virtually impossible to find a bottle of Chablis for sale. There are certainly none on the supermarket shelves, although, if you are lucky, you might find something rather dusty in a back-street grocer's.

The situation is a little better now. An increasing number of growers are selling by *vente directe* from their cellar doors, and Chablis is to be found on the wine lists of the finer restaurants of Paris and the Yonne. Until the dramatic price rises of the 1978 vintage the United States was the main export market for Chablis, but much of that market has been lost and not yet regained. There is probably little confusion between Californian Chablis and the genuine wine, as there is a considerable price difference (see the chart from Escargot's *Notebook*, 'Retail Prices, New York, 1981'[2]). Other major markets include the United Kingdom, Belgium, Holland and Germany. Some growers and *négociants* send their wine as far as Japan and South America, but more detailed information about the exports of Chablis is impossible to obtain, as the figures are always grouped with those for other white Burgundies.

There will always be a market for the finest *grands crus* and *premiers crus* Chablis, just as there is always a market and demand for the finest burgundy and claret. It is at the level of simple Chablis that the future is less certain. Chablis is competing on the same market as Pouilly Fuissé, Mâcon Blanc and the currently fashionable Sancerre, as well as the many other dry white wines, including Californian Chardonnays, that

[1] *Le Commerce des Vins de Bourgogne.*
[2] *Wine and Spirit*, July 1981.

are being made with ever-improving technical expertise and skill all over the world. Although it is true that there is a world-wide demand for dry white wine, and that the production of a couple of thousand hectares is fairly insignificant, in quantitative terms, on the world market, the *négoce* of Chablis cannot afford to be complacent.

Retail Prices, New York, 1981

$17.99	Grgich	7.99	Chablis
16.75	Chalone	7.65	St Veran
14.93	Puligny Montrachet	7.45	Mirassou, Le Franc
12.99	Mondavi	7.35	Mâcon Villages
12.45	Carneros Creek	6.82	Bgn Aligote
11.99	Trefethen	6.75	Bourgogne Bl
11.55	Meursault	6.49	Parducci
11.39	Sainte Chapelle	6.39	Sebastiani
10.75	Callaway	6.00	Paul Masson, Gallo
10.44	Pouilly Fuissé	5.49	Christian Bros
9.69	Sokol Blosser	4.95	Almadén
9.32	Chablis 1er Cru	4.89	Inglenook
9.00	Zaca Meza	3.99	Taylor
8.05	Simi		

For there is an indisputable need to promote Chablis internationally and to establish its identity in the consumer's mind. This can only be done by promotion and consumer education, which could be implemented and supported by a Comité Interprofessionnel. At present nothing is being done, but it would not be impossible to raise funds for such activities with a levy of a few centimes on each bottle as it leaves the grower or *négociant*'s cellar. This money could then be administered by a local Comité Interprofessionnel, in preference to the current situation, in which the trade pays a contribution to the Comité Interprofessionnel in Beaune, for which it receives little or nothing in return. An Office de la Promotion du Vin de Chablis does exist. It was set up in 1978 by Martin Forde, with the object of making Chablis better known and better understood on the world market, but, since his departure from Chablis, it has done little except contribute to the organization of the annual Fête du Vin.

However, Chablis does have its own wine fraternity, Les Piliers Chablisiens, whose concept and inspiration were those of Maître Sotty, the now retired *notaire* of Chablis and one of the great characters of the town. The idea came to him during a visit to Mont St Michel in 1953. In his own words, 'Je suis resté en extace dans la Crypte des Gros Piliers' ('I was in ecstasy in the Crypt of the Great Pillars'). The image of the pillars in the crypt, supporting the building, became, for him, the human pillars who supported the Chablis region and its wine. So the Piliers Chablisiens were founded. The architectural imagery was continued, for all the members have architectural titles: the founder members are 'les socles' (the pedestals); the body of members, 'les stylobates'; the head of the Piliers, 'le grand architrave'. In 1953 the condition of Chablis was sad; there had been a series of small and frost-ridden vintages and morale was low. It was imperative to find a way of arousing interest and enthusiasm in the wine and the region. The main object of the Piliers Chablisiens is to 'faire connaître' Chablis. They have an annual meeting on the fourth Sunday in November, which is combined with the annual Fête du Vin: an opportunity for the local population to taste the wines of the year. Other meetings are held throughout the year with *intronisation* ceremonies for people who have helped to promote Chablis in some way or other. Some ceremonies have taken place abroad – in Denmark, Holland and Belgium – but they are usually held at Le Petit Pontigny in Chablis. The *intronisation* ceremony takes place after a dinner at which Chablis flows freely. General hilarity ensues and the new members are required to swear fidelity to the wines of Chablis. Schoolboy pranks are played; a bald man is presented with a wig as well as his *tastevin*, and a manufacturer of bathroom suites is required to drink his toast out of a chamber pot. The festivities are concluded by traditional Burgundian singing and dancing by the Requin de Chablis. It is all very colourful and no doubt helps to spread the news of the delights of Chablis.

Jean-Claude Simmonet, resplendent in the garb of the Piliers Chablisiens

CHABLIS. - Pendant les Vendanges - La Pélée

Pour clore la cueillette du raisin, les vendangeurs ont la coutume de
avec des drapeaux et des sapins la dernière cave de raisins et de fêter d
la grappe dorée.

The traditional procession at the end of the vintage celebrates its successful
conclusion

7

A HUNDRED YEARS AND MORE
OF VINTAGES

The details of the years 1933 back to 1870 have been translated from Albert Pic's *Le Vignoble de Chablis*. The assessments of the years back to 1934 are based on conversations with various growers.

1983

With no spring frosts and fine weather at the flowering, this is a large vintage, though the exact quantity is, at the time of writing, yet to be determined. The summer was hot, but rain in August caused problems, with rot in some areas; however, the *grands crus* vineyards were unaffected. The harvest took place in perfect sunshine, to everyone's delight. It seems that the quality is good, with slightly higher acidity than in 1982.

1982

With a total of 116,897 hectolitres, this was the largest vintage ever. There was no spring frost and the flowering took place in perfect conditions. The sun continued to shine throughout the summer; there was very little rain and by mid-September the vines were laden with grapes. The resulting juice was rich and concentrated, but, with the warm summer, fairly low in acidity and high in sugar, and some rain fell during the vintage. Most people see the year as another 1979, or perhaps even better, and are pleased with the quality.

1981

Small but beautiful. Abnormal spring frosts, in areas which usually remain unaffected, caused excessive damage. Growers using aspersion apparatus suffered particularly, as the wind blew the spray away from their vines; those at Maligny suffered more than most. This setback was followed by bad weather at the flowering, which reduced the crop potential even further. The resulting yield was a mere 27 hectolitres per hectare. However, the fine summer made wines of depth and character (some say, better than any wines of the seventies) – wines to keep for at least ten years.

1980

A year that was much maligned before the vintage, with the gloom of a dull summer. In fact, the wines were much better than anticipated: not great Chablis, but classic Chablis, with good acidity and pleasantly fresh and fruity. The *premiers* and *grands crus* will develop well in bottle.

1979

The largest vintage before 1982, totalling 114,227 hectolitres, with an average yield of 77 hectolitres per hectare. The wines are easy to drink, soft, with low acidity, fruity, but with no great staying power.

1978

Another small but excellent vintage. There was no frost, but bad weather during June resulted in a prolonged, uneven flowering and a small crop. However, splendid summer weather from mid–August until the harvest in late October made wonderfully rich wines. These are wines with a concentration and intensity that will continue to develop for several years.

1977

Not a vintage to enthuse over – 'pas terrible', in the words of Guy Moreau – for the summer was poor, the harvest late and the wines high in acidity and lacking in body. Nor was the vintage large, with an average yield of 37 hectolitres per hectare. However some of the *grands crus* have developed quite pleasantly.

1976

This was the year of the long, hot summer. The grapes were ripe by the beginning of September and made full, rich wines, high in alcohol, averaging over 13°. They are low in acidity and, with this lack of balance, have developed rapidly, albeit into fine, rich wines. However, many are fading now.

1975

A year of classic Chablis, for, unlike the Côte d'Or, the region was not afflicted by climatic problems and escaped the September rains that spoilt the vintage further south. The wines have the perfect balance of fruit and acidity, without excessive alcohol. They are drinking well now – I particularly enjoyed a 1975 Les Clos from Henri Laroche at the Etoile restaurant in May 1982 – and will continue to develop well in bottle.

1974

Not highly rated among the vintages of the decade; wines without any staying power. The picking took place in the rain and the wine was low in acidity.

1973

A large volume, averaging 65 hectolitres per hectare; good-quality wines, but with the variations to be expected in a large crop. A 1973 Les Clos from Louis Pinson, drunk in May 1982, was at its peak, with depth and fruit.

1972

This was the worst vintage of the decade. Instead of spring frosts, there were frosts at the vintage, which prevented the grapes from ripening after a cool summer. Many growers waited until the second half of October to pick their grapes, but in vain. In many cases the resulting wines had more acidity than alcohol. A 1972 Chablis, tasted in May 1981 out of masochistic curiosity, was short and green.

1971

Frost at the end of April and a poor flowering reduced the yield to an average of 26 hectolitres per hectare. This, however, was compensated for by a warm summer and early autumn, so that rich, concentrated wines were made. In 1982 this long-lived vintage was reaching its peak – a Fourchaume from Henri Laroche had all the elegance and complexity associated with fine Chablis – and these wines will continue to develop over the next decade.

1970

The largest vintage before 1979, with a crop of some 74,498 hectolitres. There was no frost, followed by perfect flowering, rain in August and sunshine in September. The quality was very good, but with wines low in acidity, without any staying power. After ten years many of them are now on the downward path.

1969

Some would place this vintage higher than any of the seventies; the wines have considerable character and excellent balance.

1968

An unripe year of poor quality.

1967

Severe frost and hail greatly reduced the quantity, but the quality was good.

1966

A large crop. Some growers produced 100 hectolitres per hectare, instead of the then permitted 40 hectolitres, so that the INAO delayed the sale of the whole crop of anyone who had produced above the legal limit, until their wines could be tasted. In fact, the quality was surprisingly good: well balanced wines with a lively acidity.

1965

A disastrous summer, with equally bad wines.

1964

The grapes ripened early for a September vintage, but a twenty-four-hour torrential storm during the vintage caused considerable problems with rot, to which the fragile skins of the very ripe grapes were particularly susceptible. However, the wines that were successfully made were excellent.

1963

This was a large vintage for the period, but the quality was bad. Many of the growers had to store their wine in old *feuillettes* that had not been properly prepared, with some disastrous results. Nor was the quality helped by a poor summer.

1962

Following the excellent 1961, 1962 was decried at first and over-shadowed, but in fact the quality was excellent, with fine, elegant wines in good quantity that are continuing to show well.

1961

There was frost at Poinchy as late as 28 May, but fortunately not much harm was done. Classic Chablis was made: excellent wines, with austerity and finesse. A 1961 Chablis, Clos des Hospices, drunk in June 1982, was showing all the quality and style of a mature Chablis.

1960

A year of devastating frost, but, even so, some wine was made that was good.

1959

A very hot summer, but producing wines of better balance, with less alcohol, than the very rich 1947s. Wines of excellent quality: rich, but in small quantity.

1958

Mediocre quality, caused by problems with hail and mildew.

1957

The damage from the frost was catastrophic. The vegetation was already advanced by 10 April, when the first frosts came, and the vines had started to grow again when the second frosts came on 1 May. After that the vines gave up the unequal struggle and consequently hardly any wine was made. Robert Vocoret, for example, made just three *pièces*. The quality was described by Michel Rémon as 'execrable'. Maurice Fèvre, the father of William, made a half-muid in all, which he described as his cidroline (a play on the words cider and gasoline), 'tellement c'était mauvais'.

1956

1956 was the severest of winters. The temperature at the beginning of February fell as low as −30°C. It was impossible to work. Guy Moreau remembers having 120 half-muids of wine at Lignorelles that were completely frozen. The summer of 1956 was not much better, and the resulting wines were mediocre. No *grand cru* Chablis is to be found, as the INAO declassified the entire crop of *grands crus*, the quality being unacceptable.

1955

A year of excellent quality, with a little frost damage.

1954

Wine in abundant quantity and of average quality.

1953

Wines of good quality, but reduced in quantity by frost. Madeleine Coquard remembers that it hailed in Poinchy on Coronation Day, 2 June, but that not much damage was caused.

1952

A year of average quality and quantity.

1951

What was made was good, but frost took its toll and the crop at Poinchy was decimated by hail.

1950

Quite a good year, with what was then considered to be a large yield of 60 hectolitres per hectare: pleasantly fruity wines, but without any staying power.

1949

Excellent wines; classic Chablis.

1948

A very good year, making wines of character.

1947

One of the great Chablis vintages. A hard winter, with severe frosts; then the hot weather arrived – on 4 April. The harvest was early and the heat was such that the pickers asked for water, not wine, to drink! The grapes were rich in sugar, with little acidity, and some growers were unable to control their fermentations, with disastrous results. The more talented growers made successful, very concentrated wines, with extremely high alcohol levels. For example, Louis Pinson's Les Clos reached 15.4°, but these were wines more like Meursault than Chablis: rich, powerful wines that are still drinking well today – if you are lucky enough to find them.

1946

A year of very good quality, in small quantity.

1945

Some say there was no crop at all because of the severe frosts, and even snow on 1 May. It is, however, possible to find bottles of Chablis labelled with the 1945 vintage and, like the white wines of the Côte d'Or, these have developed into fine, mature bottles.

1940–45

The years of the German occupation are years of confusion. The vineyards were ill-cared for, because of labour shortages, and not much wine was made – certainly none of memorable quality. The vintages of 1940 and 1941 were very bad; 1942 and 1943 were average; 1944 was bad.

A 1926 poster advertising the wines of the co-operative, La Chablisienne. The use of the word *authentique* is indicative of one of Chablis' recurring problems

A quayside view of the Yonne at Auxerre, with the Abbey of Saint Germain

Old timbered houses of the sixteenth and seventeenth centuries in Auxerre

1939

The year in which war was declared is claimed to be the worst vintage in living memory. There was a foot of snow in the vineyards in October while the grapes were being picked. Indeed, one wonders why they bothered to pick them at all, as the wines were later deemed to be 'invendable'.

1938

An average year in quality and quantity.

1937

A great vintage of immense longevity. A Les Clos from the Nuits St Georges house of Lupé Cholet had a dry, nutty flavour, with a mature austerity, when tasted in June 1982.

1936

A bad year.

1935

A year of average quantity, producing rather light wines.

1934

A good year, with rich, vinous wines.

1933

A small crop. The *premier cru* vineyards were ravaged by hail. Quite good quality.

1932

Satisfactory quantity, but the persistent rain at the end of the summer prevented the complete ripening of the grapes. Ordinary quality.

1931

Good quantity; ordinary quality.

1930

The vines did not freeze, but the frequent rain resulted in continual attacks of mildew, which destroyed two-thirds of the crop. Mediocre wine.

1929

Good quantity. Excellent quality; the wines have as much alcohol as those of 1921.

1928

The frosts of May almost destroyed the whole crop, except at Lignorelles, which was spared. Exaggerated forecasts were made of the quality, causing disappointment. Prices were excessive.

1927

Frost, hail and cochylis caused serious damage, giving a crop barely larger than the previous one. Mediocre quality.

1926

The crop was greatly reduced by the frosts in May: only Lignorelles was spared. Excellent quality. The wines attained unheard of prices.

1925

Good quantity; mediocre quality.

1924

Good quantity; passable quality.

1923

Crop greatly reduced by May frosts.

1922

Abundant crop. Quality underestimated at the beginning, but the wines turned out well.

1921

Crop greatly reduced following the frosts in May, but the wines are of reasonable quality and reached a high alcoholic level.

1920

Good year for quantity; quite good for quality.

1919

Very good quantity. However, the wines, which were expected to be excellent, caused bitter disappointment, proving to be thin and of only average quality.

1917–18

Quite satisfactory yields; quite good quality.

1916

Very mediocre year for quantity and quality.

1915
Absolutely perfect quality; average quantity.

1914
Quite good quality; satisfactory quantity.

1912–13
Very mediocre years on all counts.

1911
Very little wine, but a great year.

1910
The vines did not freeze, but uninterrupted rain caused so much mildew that any treatment was totally ineffective. Complete loss of the harvest.

1909
Mediocre year on all counts.

1907–8
Quite good quantity; passable quality.

1906
An abundant crop in all surrounding areas. Unfortunately an enormous hail-storm in May destroyed nearly all the Chablis vineyards; only the right bank of the river (the first growths) was more or less spared. Perfect quality.

1905
Quite abundant crop. Mediocre wine.

1904
Good wine; satisfactory yield.

1902–3
Very mediocre years for quality and quantity.

1901
Good for quantity; passable quality. This was the last decent-sized crop produced from the old French (that is, ungrafted) vines.

1900
A very good crop in quality and quantity.

1898–9
Average quantity and quite good quality.

1897
The crop was completely destroyed by severe frost in May. No harvest.

1896
A great deal of wine, but barely passable quality.

1895
A small crop. A wine of very great quality, like that of 1893, but more *moelleux*.

1894
Abundant crop; quality only passable.

1893
A great year, in quality and quantity. Lively, perfect wine. A legendary vintage.

1892
Harvest reduced by a very hard frost in May. Good wine.

1889–91
Average years in quantity and quality.

1888
The prospects were magnificent; the vines were laden with grapes. However, continuous rain caused a violent attack of mildew, and by 1 September the vines were completely stripped of leaves; then hard early frosts occurred and the grapes, still green and unprotected by leaves, froze on the vines. A complete disaster. The little wine that it was possible to vintage was of absolutely execrable quality.

1887
An ordinary year; small in quantity.

1886
The prospects were good; but mildew, hitherto unknown in the vineyard, appeared. The growers, caught off guard, had not treated their vines, which shed their leaves prematurely. So, a barely passable year in quality and quantity.

1884–5
Very good years in quality and quantity.

1882–3
Mediocre years.

1881
Good year; excellent wine.

1880
Following the very hard winter of 1879–80 all the vines had frozen at the pruning; the growers were forced to cut them right down to the ground. There was no vintage.

1879
Very mediocre in quantity and quality.

1878
Average quantity but very good quality.

1876–7
Small harvests.

1875
An extraordinarily abundant vintage that had never been equalled. People did not know how to stock the wine and the growers in the villages were exchanging a *feuillette* of wine for an empty *feuillette*. Quality only passable: wine without value from the beginning.

1872–4
Years with hardly any crops, following the spring frosts. The vineyards were in a state of misery.

1871
Only half a crop. Quite good quality.

1870
A harvest of remarkable quality, which was unfortunately wasted following the outbreak of the Franco-Prussian war and invasion.

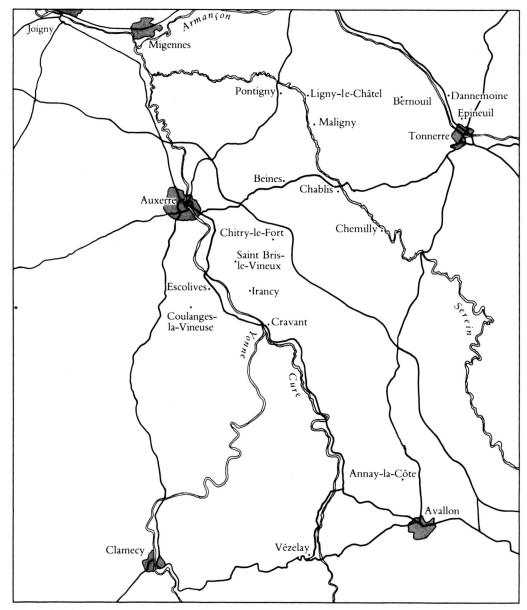

Map of the Yonne, showing the vineyards of the Auxerrois

8

'LES ANCIENS VIGNOBLES DE L'AUXERROIS': THE OTHER VINEYARDS OF THE YONNE

Today Chablis may be the best known white wine of the Yonne, but a hundred years ago, before phylloxera reached the area, the whole *département* was one of the most important wine-producing regions of France, in both the quality and quantity of its wines. Many went to quench the thirst of the Parisians, for before the advent of the railways and the easy transportation of the cheap wines of the Midi, these were the wines most commonly drunk in the capital: the *vins de comptoir* of the Parisian cafés. They are wines with a long history. Some say there were vines in the region even before the Romans. They acquired renown abroad and in the royal courts of France in the Middle Ages, and it was not until the late nineteenth century that their fortunes declined, only to experience a partial revival in the second half of the present century.

History of the Vineyards

As in so many areas of France, the Romans played an important part in the development of viticulture in the region. The Romans may actually have brought the vine with them, although Jullien[1] asserts that there were already vines in the area before they arrived. One thing, however, is certain. They gave their name to a grape variety that is found only in this part of France – the César, or Romain, and they were undoubtedly responsible for its introduction into the region. A bas-relief dating from the second or third century has been found at Escolives, a village near Coulanges-la-Vineuse; it depicts a naked *vendangeur* picking a bunch of grapes. The leaves of the vine have been identified by experts as those of the César, with their distinctive deep indentations.

Details of the development of each region will be given in the section devoted to it. Where the area as a whole is concerned, the two most significant factors were the Church and the rivers. Where there have been churches and monasteries, there have always been vines, for wine

---

[1] *Topographie des Vins de France.*

135

is essential for the eucharist. It was Saint Germain, the sixth bishop of Auxerre, who gave a particular impetus to the vineyards of Irancy, as well as to those of Auxerre itself, and both vineyards flourished during the Middle Ages under the auspices of the Abbey of Saint Germain. As we have seen in Chapter 1, where I was discussing the history of Chablis, the rivers of the region provided the means of transport and thereby helped to spread the reputation of the wines. The Yonne rises in the rugged hills of the Morvan and flows past the vineyards of Irancy, Coulanges-la-Vineuse and Saint Bris-le-Vineux to Auxerre, Joigny and Sens, before joining the Seine near Fontainebleau and so on to Paris. Tributaries of the Yonne service the other vineyards of the region: the Armançon passes Tonnerre, Epineuil and Dannemoine; the Cure and the Cousin pass Vézelay and Avallon, and the gentle Serein flows through Chablis. This navigable network of rivers, with Auxerre at its centre, gave the region its lifeline to the capital.

By the beginning of the nineteenth century the Yonne was one of the most important vineyard areas of France. Writing in 1822, Jullien[1] gives it an area of 36,000 hectares, with 4,422 communes, producing an average of 900,000 hectolitres of wine each. Of this quantity 250,000 hectolitres were drunk locally and the remaining 650,000 sent to Paris, northern France and abroad. At this time the total area in France under vines was 1,905,000 hectares, producing some 33,857,000 hectolitres of wine. The largest producing *département* was the Gironde, with 110,000 hectares of vines and an average annual production of 2,200,000 hectolitres. In comparison, the Côte d'Or had 25,000 hectares of vines, with an average annual production of 550,000 hectolitres.

Jullien classified the red wines into four categories and the whites into three. Many of the names have long since been forgotten. Among the finest of the reds were Dannemoine (with the famous slope of Olivottes), Tonnerre (with Côtes de Pitoy, Côtes de Perrière and Côtes de Préaux) and Auxerre (with the hill called La Grande Côte d'Auxerre). In Auxerre, La Chainette and Migraine were particularly mentioned: La Chainette (five hectares) 'produces generous wine, fine and delicate, with vigour and a pleasant bouquet'. Migraine (twenty hectares) is less delicate 'with more body and alcohol, which allows it to travel'. And so the wines of Auxerre and Tonnerre dominate the best category. In the second category, there are more wines from the Grande Côte d'Auxerre, with names like Judas, Pied de Rat and Quétard. Epineuil is

---

[1] *Topographie de Tous les Vignobles Connus.*

mentioned, with now extinct vineyard names, as is Irancy (with Palotte and other picturesque names, like Paradis and Bergère), and at Coulanges-la-Vineuse a property called Seigneur also features. In the third class there are more wines from Auxerre, Vincelottes, Avallon, Clos at Vézelay, Saint Jacques at Joigny and La Vieille Plante at Pontigny. The red wines of Saint Bris-le-Vineux are not mentioned until we come to the fourth class, together with a host of long-obscure names from Vermenton, Pouilly, Môlesme and Paron near Sens.

Not surprisingly, in the first category of the whites there is Chablis, but first Jullien mentions Tonnerre, the Côtes de Vaumorillon and, in particular, Grisées, as approaching the quality of Meursault. His classification of Chablis is discussed in Chapter 1, but it is interesting to see that he mentions Saint Bris-le-Vineux in the second category and Bernouil, where pre-phylloxera wines are still grown, in the third category.

Writing five years after Jullien, Cavoleau[1] is slightly at variance with him over the total area of vineyards. He gives a figure of 33,630 hectares and divides them as follows:

	hectares	hectolitres
Auxerre, including Irancy, Chablis, Coulanges-la-Vineuse, St Bris-le-Vineux	13,960	406,268
Avallon	4,000	83,200
Joigny	6,083	142,324
Sens	4,270	117,870
Tonnerre, including Epineuil	5,317	136,942

In 1868 Dr Jules Guyot[2] gives a total of 38,000 hectares, of which only 2,000 were planted with Pinot Noir, Blanc and Gris, to give the best wines. The other 36,000 hectares were planted with vines of high yields: Tressot or Verrot, Romain, César or Picorneau, Epicier or Gois, Gamay à Grains Ronds and Gamay à Grains Ovales. Their yields were double that of the Pinot (40 hectolitres per hectare, as opposed to 20 hectolitres), and their price was half (25 francs per hectolitre, as opposed to 50 francs for the Pinot).

[1] *Oenologie Française.*
[2] *Etude des Vignobles de France.*

The vine at that time accounted for a third of the agricultural production of the Yonne and 38,000 families, about half the population of the *département*, were involved in viticulture. Guyot then adds sombrely that 'the fine growths of Lower Burgundy, except for Chablis, are nearly all in desperate straits, especially in Tonnerre and the Auxerrois'. Sadly, during the nineteenth century an increasing number of high-yielding, low-quality vines were planted, to meet the demand from Paris for cheap wine. As early as 1816 Jullien says, 'it would be desirable to renew the decree of Charles IX, who forbade the planting of the infamous Gamay in the vineyards which were producing fine wines'.[1] He is referring to an attempt in the late sixteenth century to restore some order to the vineyards of the Côte d'Or. But the damage had been done: inferior varieties, such as Lombard, Gois and Damery became established in vineyards that were rapidly losing their quality and reputation.

The vineyards were then attacked by mildew and ravaged by phylloxera, which first appeared in the Yonne in 1887. Although the remedy for phylloxera of grafting French vines onto American rootstock had been suggested as early as 1869 and was becoming more widely accepted by the end of the 1880s, the first graftings were not made in the Yonne until 1897 and many of the vineyards were never replanted. Twenty years later the First World War decimated the local population.

Again, as with the vineyards of Chablis, the lure of the capital caused further rural depopulation and, what with the unequal struggle to compete with the cheap wines of the Midi, the incentive to replant and restore the vineyards was gone. By 1930 the 40,000 hectares of the 1880s had fallen to 8,950 hectares. Vineyards like Irancy and Coulanges-la-Vineuse fell into further disrepute in the 1930s and 1940s, when hybrid varieties were grown, simply for the benefit of the local population.

Over the past twenty years, however, there have been the gentle stirrings of a renaissance. Vines are being planted on the slopes of Vézelay, at Saint Père-sur-Vézelay and Fontette. At Epineuil there are definite signs of a revival. At Joigny one enthusiastic family continues the vinous traditions. Coulanges-la-Vineuse is returning to a noble grape variety, and the red wines of Irancy and the white wines of Saint-Bris-le-Vineux and Chitry-le-Fort are flourishing. In Auxerre,

---

[1] *Topographie des Vins de France.*

however, all that remains of the once famous Grande Côte is the protected vineyard of La Chainette.

In 1980 there were 3,300 hectares of vines in the region, of which 2,324 hectares produce wines of *appellation contrôlée*, or VDQS, quality. The remaining 976 hectares are without status, producing *vin de consommation courante*, the everyday drinking wine for the families of those who make them. A partial decline in the area under vines continues, but it is only in these nameless vineyards. The area of *appellation contrôlée* vineyards is now increasing and today there are rays of hope on the horizon. Pockets of vines in once-famous vineyards are coming to life again and the future can once again be looked forward to with optimism.

Before we consider each area, with its individual history, character and current conditions, some account should be given of two organizations which play an important part in the wine trade of the region.

There has been a long tradition of sparkling wine in the Auxerrois. Both Sacy and Aligoté, with their high acidity and low alcohol, make ideal base wines for sparkling wine. Before the days of *appellation contrôlée* it was not uncommon for some of this wine to find its way to Epernay and Reims, as did some Chablis. Then it found its outlet in Germany and was bought by companies like Henkell for the production of Sekt. However, with the floating of the Deutschmark in 1970, the demand from Germany fell dramatically, and so the growers had to find their own means to sell their wine. This situation led to the forming of the Société d'Interêt Collectif Agricole du Vignoble Auxerrois – or SICAVA, as it is more generally called – in 1972. This organization was founded at the instigation of one of the principal growers of Saint Bris-le-Vineux, Michel Esclavy, who is still its president. Its premises are at Bailly, a tiny hamlet on the banks of the Yonne, where there are enormous caves in the hillsides. These were originally quarried to provide stone for the Panthéon in Paris, and were then used as mushroom caves, before becoming wine cellars, for which they are ideal, with a natural temperature of 12°.

The purpose of the SICAVA is to make and market the sparkling wine that is no longer required in Germany. It is not a co-operative. Shares in the organization are bought by two categories of investors: the local growers, and people associated in the wine trade in some other way who may be *négociants* or transporters, and do not necessarily live in the region. The growers deliver a certain percentage of their grape production, rather than must, according to the size of their shareholding. It is usually about 15 per cent and they are paid according to the weight of their grapes at a price determined before the vintage, in the same way as in Champagne. They are subsequently allowed to take back a part of their wine to sell under their own names. Those members who did not contribute to the production receive dividends in the normal way, depending on the commercial situation.

It is not easy to join the SICAVA, and – as with La Chablisienne – once one has become a member it is even more difficult to withdraw, as the organization demands a serious commitment on the part of the growers, which is embodied in the terms of entry. The majority of the growers come from Chitry and Saint Bris, as the two main producers of white grapes in the area. The new members (mainly from Coulanges and Irancy) are allotted shares on less favourable terms than the founder members, as they did not have to run the initial risks. However, the organization does encourage young growers to join, and it offers all the growers who are members the assurance of an income from their grapes and of a market for their wine. It is rare for a grower to give all his crop to the SICAVA; most use some to make their own still wine.

The sole product of the SICAVA is Crémant de Bourgogne, which became an appellation in 1975, with the object of replacing Bourgogne Mousseux. The method is that of Champagne, with quite modern machinery and manual *remuage*. The differences between the styles of wine come from the grapes and the soil. The main grape varieties are Aligoté, Sacy, Chardonnay, Pinot Noir (which is used for both white and rosé) and Gamay (for rosé alone). The exact proportions vary from year to year, but at least 45 per cent is Aligoté. The different styles are (in white) Brut de Brut (which is made from the best *cuvées*, with no additional dosage), Brut, Sec and Demi Sec, and (in rosé, which was introduced in 1979) Brut and Demi Sec. No Blanc de Blancs or red sparkling wine is made. Brut is by far and away the most important, accounting for 80 per cent of the market. Appellation regulations dictate a minimum of nine months' bottle age, but the SICAVA tries to give its wines eighteen months' to two years' ageing, depending on demand. Its wines are sold under the brand name of Meurgis – meaning, in local *patois*, *petits murs*, the small stone walls found in the vineyards.

The main market of the SICAVA is in Burgundy itself: it sells to *négociants*, who in turn sell the wine under their own labels. Some wine is exported, but the SICAVA sees its main competitors as being the other sparkling wine houses of the Côte d'Or. Undoubtedly it has benefited from the recent difficulties of supply in Champagne, but it has also been adversely affected by small crops.

The value of the SICAVA seems to be generally accepted by the growers of the Auxerrois. It was created at a time when the region was fraught with commercial difficulties, having lost its traditional market. It also provided a use, and a uniformity, to the hotch-potch of grape varieties grown in the area. Above all, it gives its members a sense of commitment and an economic strength. For André Sorin it is 'la porte de sortie' for the wines of the Auxerrois. A few growers, however, feel that it takes away their independence and they prefer to find their own markets.

Like most other wine regions, the vineyards of the Auxerrois have their own *confrérie*: Les Trois Ceps. This was founded in 1965, and the three *ceps*, or vines, were originally Irancy, Saint-Bris-le-Vineux and Chitry-le-Fort; but now other areas have joined: Clos de la Chainette in Auxerre, Coulanges-la-Vineuse, Vézelay and Joigny. Their annual festival, La Fête des Vins de l'Yonne (generally known as La Fête du Sauvignon), takes place on the Sunday before 11 November in Saint Bris. There are wines galore from each area to be tasted, and a *bal populaire* and other *folklorique* entertainments. In March the *confrères* meet for a Banquet de Saint Vincent in the cellars of the SICAVA, and the patron saint of the wine-maker is feted on 22 January with Les Tournants Saint Vincent – a moving feast hosted by a different commune each year.

Bernouil

The INAO has never fully defined or classified the vineyards of the Yonne; throughout the *département* there are pockets of vines that are entitled to the appellation of Bourgogne, provided that they are cultivated and the wine is produced in a manner conforming to the regulations of the appellation. The final test of quality is the annual *labellisation* tasting.

One of the more interesting such vineyards is at Bernouil, which once upon a time was one of the eighty or so villages whose wines were covered by the umbrella name of Chablis. Today it produces Bourgogne Blanc. There is nothing unusual in that, but the vines are pre-phylloxera, which is somewhat out of the ordinary. For the soil at Bernouil is particularly sandy, and for this reason the phylloxera louse never gained a foothold.

Robert Forgeot, who is really a farmer making his living from cows and wheat, also has 1.2 hectares of ungrafted Chardonnay vines. He says they are two hundred years old; certainly they have the thick gnarled trunks of old vines. Originally there were many more ungrafted vines in the village, but they were pulled up during the Second World War because of labour shortage and lack of interest. Forgeot, however, kept his because he liked them, which is as good a reason as any.

He makes his wine in a small cellar under his house, keeping it in old oak barrels; apart from a light filtration before bottling by a mobile machine from Mâcon, he does not treat it at all. The resulting wine is not especially remarkable, but Forgeot has a small following of private customers and has also supplied cuttings to other growers in the region.

Chitry-le-Fort

If you approach Chitry-le-Fort from Courgis and Chablis, you are greeted first by the sight of the imposing church, with its solid square tower. As its name suggests, Chitry was once a fortified town, and in the Middle Ages the main street, and almost only street, La Grande Rue, formed the boundary between the lands of the Count of Tonnerre in Champagne and the Count of Auxerre in Burgundy.

The vineyards themselves are not immediately visible as you approach Chitry: they are either on the slopes towards Saint Bris and face south or south-west, or on a large plateau with a westerly aspect. Little is known of their history. Certainly Chitry was one of the villages whose wines were sold under the name of Chablis in the last century. The Tribunal d'Auxerre of 1929 accorded its wine the name of Bourgogne des Environs de Chablis; the term Chablis Village was also permitted at one time, but all reference to Chablis was forbidden once the appellation of Chablis was more strictly defined.

Today Chitry is one of the four viticultural communes of the Auxerrois, producing (like its neighbour, Saint Bris-le-Vineux) an assortment of grape varieties and wines: Chardonnay, Sacy, Aligoté, Pinot Noir, Gamay and Sauvignon. It suffered the same changes of fortune as the other villages of the Auxerrois – the same sharp decline in the vineyard area caused by phylloxera and rural depopulation – and was at its lowest ebb in the mid-1950s, with less than a hundred hectares of vines. Since then vines have been planted on land that was once used for grazing and cereals. There have been a consolidation of the vineyards into small family holdings and a fall in the number of growers. The cherry-trees, too, are less important.

As in Saint Bris, the creation of the SICAVA has made an enormous difference to the viability of the vineyards of Chitry, by providing the main outlet for its wines. White Bourgogne Grand Ordinaire is disappearing, and most Sacy goes to the SICAVA to be turned into Crémant de Bourgogne. Gamay is used for red Bourgogne Grand Ordinaire. Pinot Noir was also planted, as in Saint Bris in the early 1970s, when sales of white wine were slow. However, it only grows successfully on the best south-facing slopes and is now of little significance.

For most people Aligoté is the most important variety in terms of production, but most consider Bourgogne Blanc made from Chardonnay to be Chitry's best wine. Not unnaturally, the local growers compare their Chardonnay to that of Chablis: 'Il vaut le Chablis' ('It's worth the same as Chablis'). For Chitry is in the canton of Chablis, its vineyards are on the same kimmeridgian soil as Chablis, and the methods of production used in both places are identical. There is, however, a difference, which comes from the positions of the vineyards: those of Courgis, the adjoining village to Chitry, are part of the valley of the Serein and therefore within the confines of Chablis; those of Chitry form part of the valley of the Yonne and are not. The dividing line is the motorway under which you pass between Courgis and Chitry. For some growers in Chitry their interest in Chablis is not confined to ineffective comparisons. A few have participated in the expansion of Chablis and now have vineyards in the villages of Beines, Préhy and Courgis. As yet their vineyards are rather new and I have the impression that it is not as easy for them to sell Chablis as the cheaper wines of Chitry. Prices tend to depend upon the state of the Chablis market: the price of Bourgogne Blanc from Chitry will vary according to the price of Chablis. There is perhaps a certain jealousy of the prosperity and success of the neighbouring vineyard. As one grower from Chitry put it, 'Eux [the people of Chablis], ils ont des cravates, et nous, nous n'en avons pas' ('They wear ties; we don't').

Sauvignon is not widely grown in Chitry. Only a few growers produce it and they are often people who, through family contacts, have land in Saint Bris as well. However, there is a difference between the Sauvignon of the two villages – a difference that is attributable to the soil composition. There is a much higher percentage of limestone in the soil of Chitry, which produces a Sauvignon that is much less obvious, or *typé*, in its youth than that of Saint Bris and, contrary to general belief, is capable of ageing and developing into a wine of considerable depth. On the other hand, a Sauvignon produced on portlandian soil is very perfumed as a young wine, but lacks the staying power of a wine of kimmeridgian provenance.

The growers of Chitry are organized in a Syndicat de la Défense des Vins de Chitry, which forms part of the Groupement des Syndicats Auxerrois. The main preoccupation at the moment is with the labelling of their wines. Most use the name Côtes de Chitry, a term which is not strictly allowed by the INAO. Naturally the growers would prefer a more formal and permanent appellation to describe the 120 hectares of vineyards in the village, which have not yet even been conclusively delimited by the INAO.

Viticultural methods do not differ from practice elsewhere in the Auxerrois. Chardonnay is pruned as in Chablis, and for the other varieties the *guyot* system (single or double, according to the grower's preference and the grape variety) is used. There is nothing distinctive about the vinification methods and no one has any very sophisticated equipment. The Pinot Noir is usually aged for a few months in old oak barrels; those who bottle their wines tend, more often than not, to postpone doing so until an order arrives.

Three-quarters of the growers of Chitry belong to the SICAVA. Some give all their production to be transformed into sparkling wine; others sell in bulk to the *négoce* of Chablis or Beaune. Out of a total of thirty-five growers in Chitry, just over twenty sell some of their wine in bottle. Very little of their wine reaches foreign markets. I visited three of the larger growers, who are fairly typical of the village: Paul Colbois, Joel Griffe and Roland Viré.

Paul Colbois
Paul Colbois inherited a little land from his parents, but has basically created his own vineyard, which now consists of ten hectares of Aligoté, Sauvignon, Chardonnay and Pinot Noir (forming the basic burgundy appellations), as well as a little Chablis at Beines. His son Daniel is typical of a young grower in Chitry in concentrating on Chablis, with fifteen hectares in the new vineyards at Beines. Like other Chitry growers, Paul Colbois also has a few hectares of cherry-trees. His methods and equipment are unsophisticated.

Joel Griffe
Joel Griffe is president of the *syndicat* of Chitry. He is a straightforward, down-to-earth, youngish man, who inherited his vineyards from his

The village of Irancy, nestling in the valley, in the spring. Cherry trees are almost as important as vines in the area

Vintage time on the Côte Saint Jacques, with the town of Joigny and the
Yonne in the background

grandfather. However, there have been Griffes in Chitry since the Middle Ages.

His seven-hectare vineyard is made up of 85 ares of Sauvignon, 2.5 hectares of Sacy (which all goes to the SICAVA), 2.5 hectares of Aligoté, a hectare of Pinot Noir and 50 ares of Gamay. He uses enamel-lined vats and ages his red wine in wood for two years. His whites are bottled six to twelve months after the vintage. It was his 1969 Sauvignon de Saint Bris that completely changed my preconceived ideas that Sauvignon does not age. By September 1982 it had developed a character more akin to Chardonnay than Sauvignon, with a rather nutty, leafy nose and palate and plenty of fruit and flavour.

Roland Viré
Roland Viré is a quiet, serious man, whose methods are traditional. He inherited a few vines from his parents, but has basically created his vineyard himself since the war. He owns ten hectares of vines, growing a little of this and a bit of that: Aligoté, Sacy (for Bourgogne Grand Ordinaire and Crémant de Bourgogne), Gamay (for Bourgogne Grand Ordinaire), Pinot Noir (for Bourgogne Rouge) and a little Bourgogne Rosé, Chardonnay (for Bourgogne Blanc) and Sauvignon. Half of his production goes to the SICAVA; the other half he bottles himself and sells mainly from his cellar door. He works in rather quaint old cellars under his house in the main square of Chitry. Chitry does not have such magnificent cellars as Saint Bris, since the village is in a valley and too close to the water-table.

Other growers whose names you may find on labels are listed below:

Noel Aubron	Gérard Griffe
Léon Berthelot	Noel Joudelat
Aimé Chalmeau	Michel Morin
Edmond Chalmeau	Roger Race
Marcel Chalmeau	Jacques Raoul
Daniel Colbois	Jean Raoul
Michel Colbois	Régis Richoux
Jean Démeaux	Marcel Sichon
Gilbert Giraudon	Henri Total

Coulanges-la-Vineuse

The small town of Coulanges-la-Vineuse stands on the opposite side of the valley from Irancy; the Yonne is crossed at Vincelottes. It is a town of narrow, winding streets, which once clustered behind fortifications. The vineyards are on the undulating hillsides to the south-west of the town, with a south-east aspect.

The town's origins are Roman; its long vinous tradition is inherent in its name. Historically, it differs from Irancy in that the development of its vineyards depended not on the church, but on the local landowners. For this reason perhaps the best known vineyard of Coulanges was called Clos de Seigneur. In 1777 Claude Courtepée[1] described the wine of Coulanges as being 'finer, lighter and with a more delicate vigour than that of Irancy'. Several French kings favoured Coulanges – Charles V, Charles VI, Louis XI and Henri IV – and Coulanges was also one of the wines recommended to Louis XIV by his doctor.

In 1676 an immense fire destroyed three-quarters of the town; the church was burnt down and twenty-two wine presses were lost. There was not enough water to quench the fire – Coulanges has always been short of water – but Mme de Villefranche 'had thirty barrels of wine broken open and the wine thrown on the flames to stop the disaster'. Hyppolyte Ribière, who wrote a history of the town in 1851, says, 'At Coulanges wine provides everything and pays for everything, even the water they drink.' So it would seem that Coulanges certainly merits its epithet La Vineuse.

However, its wines have not always been renowned for their quality. Jullien[2] placed the best of them, Clos de Seigneur, in his second category. The owner had kept the Franc Pinot vines, so that the wine was as good as that of Irancy. Elsewhere, however, Gammé (Gamay) and Célar had been widely planted, with the consequent deleterious effect on quality. In 1857 Rendu[3] says that Coulanges is 'a vineyard of quantity rather than quality', producing 'a simple ordinaire'. Guyot confirmed that the 'famous Pinot is still grown but is tending to disappear'.[4] César or Romain were more commonly found.

[1] *Histoire Abrégée du Duché de Bourgogne.*
[2] *Topographie de Tous les Vignobles Connus.*
[3] *Ampelographie Française.*
[4] Op. cit.

Like the other vineyards of the Auxerrois, Coulanges suffered from the effects of phylloxera, and, faced with the competition of wines from the Midi, the growers had little incentive to replant the rather mediocre vineyards. From about eight hundred hectares before the phylloxera crisis, the vineyards declined dramatically, and cherry-trees took over in importance in the town's economy.

Historically, comparisons can be made with Irancy. However, in Coulanges the revival of the vineyards and the replanting with fine grape varieties came much later than in Irancy. It is only in the last ten or twenty years that Pinot Noir has replaced the hybrids in the vineyards of Coulanges, and, with only sixty hectares of vines, the vineyards have by no means regained their former importance. Cherry-trees and farmland still abound.

The main grape variety is Pinot Noir. Before the advent of phylloxera both César and Tressot were grown, but they have now disappeared from the area and the elegant wines of Coulanges come exclusively from Pinot Noir. Earlier in the century, even the future of the Pinot Noir was uncertain; it was threatened by various types of Gamay, not only Gamay à Jus Blanc, but Teinturier varieties such as Gamay de Chaudenay. It was the grower Serge Hugot's father who realized the significance of Pinot Noir in maintaining the quality of Coulanges wine; during the Second World War (when hybrid varieties were being planted, in order to produce wine in large quantities, but of questionable quality) he kept his vineyard of Pinot Noir. Fortunately his example has been followed by other growers, and Pinot Noir is once again well established in the vineyards of Coulanges.

Most of the growers still have a small proportion of Gamay à Jus Blanc, which is used to make Bourgogne Grand Ordinaire. There is also a little Aligoté in the area, but not in any significant quantity. Nobody has vineyards of any great size; the largest family holding is just over eight hectares, which is not sufficient to make a living purely from vines. Polyculture is the norm; most people grow crops and also have orchards of cherry-trees. There is a considerable amount of land which is covered with cherry orchards, but which could be replanted with vines. As in Saint Bris, the future of the cherry-trees is uncertain.

Frost is not a great problem in Coulanges, partly because it is only the less frost-prone sites that have remained as vineyards and partly because the area is less susceptible to frost in any case. In fact, here, as in other vineyards of the Auxerrois, frost protection on the scale of that carried out at Chablis would be financially impossible: the growers can only hope for the best. Pruning is done by the *taille guyot* (or single *guyot*) method and most vines are grafted onto SO4 rootstocks in the calcareous soil. Otherwise, viticultural methods do not differ from those used elsewhere in the Auxerrois.

Coulanges is often compared to Irancy. The exposure of the vineyards is, however, different: south-west for Irancy, and south-east for Coulanges, which does not, therefore, have quite the same intensity of sunshine as Irancy. There are also slight differences in the soil. On the other hand, methods of vinification do not vary greatly; possibly the only difference is that the wine is kept on the skins for a shorter time at Coulanges. Both oak and chestnut barrels are used – there seems to be little difference between the two (Serge Hugot, for instance, has both) – as well as enamel-painted and fibreglass-lined cement vats. His wine spends seven or eight months in wood after the malolactic fermentation is finished. He usually bottles his wine about fourteen months after the vintage. Rosé is even more uncommon at Coulanges than at Irancy and is usually made only in years of a large vintage, such as 1979.

Officially, under the decree of 1937, Coulanges is entitled only to the appellation of Bourgogne, but the addition of the name Coulanges-la-Vineuse on the label has, in effect, been unofficially tolerated. The situation needs to be clarified.

Although Coulanges is re-establishing its reputation, and the vineyard area has expanded over the last two decades, with the possibility of yet more expansion, the prospects for flourishing production in Coulanges are still uncertain. For there is a shortage of young people willing to take over the existing vineyards, and a lack of outside interest in the area. It is unlikely that the vineyards of Coulanges will ever be as productive as those of Saint Bris or Irancy. There are only eleven *viticulteurs* in Coulanges – not many for an area which considers itself essentially to be a wine community. The underlying doubts about the future are understandable.

Most of the growers of Coulanges sell a proportion of their wines to the *négociants* of Chablis, and it is under those labels that Coulanges will be found on the export market, if at all. Henri Laroche, under their Bacheroy Josselin label, make an attractive Coulanges, as does Simmonet Febvre.

Although Coulanges is lighter in style than Irancy, it is a wine that will age. The year 1947 was an exceptional vintage; 1952, 1959, 1969, 1976 and 1978 are also considered to be years of note. Certainly Serge Hugot's 1978 is a wine that I shall long remember.

At Migé, a village outside Coulanges, there is one of the remaining old wine presses of the region. It was found at Coulanges in a state of disrepair, together with a book recording the weight and quantity of wines produced each year. It is now maintained by Monsieur Raboulin, the former Mayor of Migé.

I visited the most important growers: Raymond Dupuis, Serge Hugot, André Martin et Fils and Pierre Vigreux.

Raymond Dupuis
Raymond Dupuis comes from an old Coulanges family which dates back to at least 1700, and his cellars, with their solid arches, are probably as old. He is president of the Syndicat des Viticulteurs. He has six hectares of vines: five of Pinot Noir (for Bourgogne Rouge) and one of Gamay (for Bourgogne Grand Ordinaire). His wines are generally well-considered; his 1979 Coulanges-la-Vineuse, tasted in December 1981, had a delicious Pinot Noir flavour, slightly reminiscent of raspberries, and with some weight.

Serge Hugot
Quite the best Coulanges I have ever tasted came from Serge Hugot. His father and grandfather were growers before him, and it is due to his father that Coulanges kept Pinot Noir in the vineyards at all. We talked over a bottle of his 1978, which is a wine of greater depth, character and weight than many others. Hugot ascribes this to the fact that his vineyard has the best aspect of all the vineyards of Coulanges, for it faces south-west, rather than south-east, and so his grapes are riper.

André Martin et Fils
André Martin and his son are relative newcomers to the region, as they only began planting vines in 1956. Now, however, they have the largest vineyard holding in Coulanges, with eight hectares of Pinot Noir and 1.5 of Gamay.

Pierre Vigreux
Pierre Vigreux is a smiling, ruddy-faced man, who, immediately on my arrival, suggested that we went into the cellar to talk 'pour se mettre dans l'ambiance', and there we drank his lightly perfumed 1979 Coulanges while we talked. He is not only a *viticulteur*, but also a farmer, and has only three hectares of vines: of Pinot Noir and Gamay. However, his family have been *viticulteurs* for centuries and genera-

tions. He views his fellow-growers with friendly objectivity. They are, he considers, generally reluctant to try out new ideas; for instance, it was he who was the first to use weed-killer on his crops. 'On sort des temps préhistoriques.' He uses old port barrels made of chestnut to age his wine. His cellars are built against the old fortifications of Coulanges.

The other growers whose names may appear on a bottle of Coulanges are as follows:

Maxime Auguste
Maurice Bernard, Père et Fils
Edouard Chambard
Henri Dupuis

Henri Hervin, Père et Fils
Maurice and Pierre Ledoux
Jean Lemoule

La Grande Côte d'Auxerre

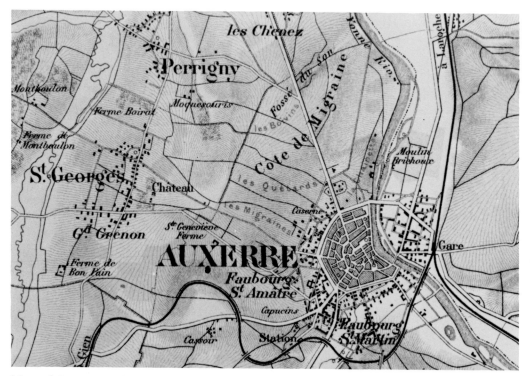

Map of Auxerre (*Atlas Vinicole*, 1901)

The wines of Auxerre have had a long history and enjoyed a reputation even older than that of the wines of the Côte d'Or. The earliest mention of them, and of the somewhat appropriately named Clos de Migraine, was in 680, when Bishop Virgile of Auxerre described the vineyards at the foot of the city walls. In the tenth century the monk and poet Héric began his description of the town in the *Vie de Saint Germain d'Auxerre* with the words 'of the goodness of its wine'.

A century later it was said of the Count of Gatinois that he had at Auxerre 'vines that produced a wine that was delicious beyond words'. Henri d'Andeli, in his twelfth-century fable in verse, *La Bataille des Vins*, mentioned Chablis, Auxerre and Tonnerre among the seventy most famous growths of France, and at the same period Chrétien de Troyes, in his *Roman de Perceval*, made his hero drink the 'bons vins d'Aucerre et de Soissons'.

By the Middle Ages the fame of the wines of Auxerre had spread abroad. No mention was as yet made of Beaune and Bordeaux, but adjectives like *superlativum* and *pretiosissimum* were used to describe the wines of Auxerre. By 1184 the town of Auxerre was able to buy certain privileges – in particular, an important and rare one at the time, 'la liberté des vendanges'.

In 1203 King John was given a *tonneau* of Auxerre wine in gratitude for affixing a royal seal to an act confirming an agreement between the Earl of Leicester and the Bishop of Lincoln. He must have liked the wine, for in 1212 he is recorded as having purchased a further twenty-six barrels. Records exist of a Rouen merchant, Martin de la Pommerange, sending six ships to England during the reign of Henry III, laden with wines from the Ile de France and Auxerre.

In 1245 a Franciscan monk from Ferrara, Fra Salimbène, wrote,

When Brother Gabriel from Cremona assured me one day that Auxerre alone had more vineyards and vines than Cremona, Parma, Reggio and Modena together, I marvelled and thought it incredible. But when I dwelt myself at Auxerre, I saw he had said the truth; for not only are the hillsides covered with vineyards, but the level plain also, as I have seen with my own eyes. For the men of that land sow not, nor do they reap, nor have they storehouse or barn; but they send wine to Paris by the river which flows hard by, and there they sell it for a noble price, which provides them entirely with food and clothing.

According to Abbé Leneuf, writing in 1322, by this time there were so many vines at Auxerre that it was necessary to increase the number of presses in the town. It was also recorded in the same year that 'the brokers and wine trade were among the most important occupations of the town'.

The wines of Auxerre were favoured by two kings of France. François I, in Patent Letters of 1522, allowed 'la vente libre dans tout le royaume du vin récolté d'Auxerre', and Henri IV suppressed taxes on the wines of Auxerre. He has the reputation of enjoying wines from all over France, but his everyday drinking wines, 'son ordinaire', were the wines of Irancy, Coulanges and Auxerre. English kings also continued to favour Auxerre. Henry VIII and Thomas Cromwell bought Auxerre wines in 1536; these were taken by river to Rouen and were then shipped to London.

Rabelais, that famous epicurean, extolled the virtues of the wines of Auxerre in the sixteenth century, and in 1606 a M. Sicard sang in his *Airs à Boire*:

> De tout le bon vin Bourguignon
> Je diray mon advis sans peine
> Je n'en trouve point de si bon
> Que l'excellent vin de Migraine
>
> De tout le bon vin d'Auxerrois
> Celuy-ci remporte la gloire.

('Of all the good wines of Burgundy, I will say my opinion, without hesitation. I do not find any as good as the excellent wine of Migraine. Of all the good wine of the Auxerrois, that one reaps glory.')

In 1648 merchants of Auxerre were recorded as selling wine at the Porte Saint Bernard in Paris – wine which they had transported by boat. There is also evidence of Parisians owning vineyards in the Auxerrois. As early as 1222 Guillaume Bourdin had given the Hôtel-Dieu in Paris the ten *arpents* of vines that he owned in Auxerre. Four centuries later Toussaint Bourdillat had three *arpents* of vines at Vermenton and the writer Nicholas Boileau Despréaux owned five *arpents* of Vaumorillon near Tonnerre. These Parisians preferred the wines of Auxerre and Chablis to the often green wines of Paris itself, and, with the availability of the navigable river network, there was no problem in bringing their crop to the capital.

An amusing reference is provided in 1725 by M. Arnoux, a Frenchman living in England, who does not support the common view on the quality of the wines of Auxerre:

I am now going to treat concerning all the Vineyards of Upper Burgundy; those who have pass'd the grand Road that leads from Dijon to Lyon, the length of the Hills will do justice to my exactness and I desire those that have not yet been there, to believe that this Relation is agreeable to Truth. I have a hundred times heard Boasting of the wines of many Hills near Auxerre, to which they give the Name of the Wine of Burgundy. It is true those hills are in Burgundy, but they are 90 miles distant from the true Hills, of which I spoke just now, which only produce these wines of Burgundy which are in Reputation and which they drink after two Manners, by the Nose and by the Mouth, either both at once or separately; both at once in that when one drinks them the Pleasure which he has in the smell vies with the Relish it has on the Palate, and separately so that a Person that has been used to drink it, may know whether it be the true Burgundy or not by the smell or sweet Odour. The Good Tasters taste it by the Nose, before they put it to their Mouths and all the other climates of Burgundy, as those of Chablis and Auxerre have no such Quality as the true wines of Burgundy have, although they are really made and produced there.[1]

This opinion is refuted in 1807 by Grimod de la Reynière.[2] He refers to 'Lower Burgundy, the Côte d'Auxerre, Clos de l'Evesque and Clos des Bénédictins, the wine of Villeneuve which needs a good year, Coulanges that warms the throat, Vermenton and Avallon, the best wines. You find them in Paris at the honest M. Barbier in the rue Bailitte, wines from Vincelottes, Migrenne[3] and la Chainette. For everyday drinking these wines from Lower Burgundy are more wholesome than those of Upper Burgundy.'

In the nineteenth century La Grande Côte d'Auxerre enjoyed a fine reputation. Migraine and La Chainette feature near the top of Jullien's classification, and other forgotten names, such as Pied de Rat, Judas and Quétard, appear in the second category. In 1868 Guyot describes these wines as the pride of Lower Burgundy. Vineyards covered the hillsides outside Auxerre to the east of the town. The vines were two-thirds

[1] *Dissertation sur la situation de Bourgogne.*
[2] *Journal des Gourmands et des Belles*, Vol. IV.
[3] An old spelling for Migraine.

Pinot, one-sixth Tressot and one-sixth Romain. At the height of the region's fame in the nineteenth century there were 138 hectares of vines; today there are just three. The small vineyard of Clos de la Chainette is all that remains of a once glorious vineyard.

La Chainette owes its survival to its ownership by a public institution. Until the Revolution it was in the hands of the monks of the Abbey of Saint Germain; it then had a brief spell of ownership by some local bourgeois, before being sold to the Hôpital Psychiatrique de l'Yonne. Today the vineyard is protected, and so there is no risk of the land being encroached upon for building purposes. Indeed, it is surrounded by hospital buildings and the sprawling town of Auxerre.

It is perhaps sad that the famous wines of Auxerre were red, while today La Chainette produces only white and rosé wines. The vineyard is planted half with Chardonnay and half with Pinot Noir; as the production is so small, it would not be feasible to change to red.

The vineyard enjoys its own microclimate; it is very sheltered and warm, as it is surrounded by buildings, and so the vegetation can be as much as eight to ten days ahead of the rest of the Yonne. When the *ban de vendange* is issued, the grapes are usually very ripe, and they are picked very quickly, sometimes with the help of the patients at the hospital.

M. Viault, who is responsible for the *service agricole* of the hospital, runs the vineyard and its cellars, as well as a farm outside Auxerre. His vinification methods are traditional. The rosé is fermented on the skins for from six to twenty-four hours, depending on the conditions of the individual vintage. No wood is used and the cellars are heated to ensure that the malolactic fermentation occurs. The tartrates precipitate naturally during the winter and the wines are usually bottled in the July following the vintage. It is all rather unsophisticated; there is a small cellar, with wooden casks that are no longer used, but kept for visual effect, and one of the largest spider's webs I have ever seen was hanging from the beams.

The results are two very pleasant wines: a rosé with infinitely more fruit than the average rosé, and a white with a light Chardonnay character. Both have been *Appellation Bourgogne contrôlée* since 1942. The wines have a small following, both locally and throughout France; regular customers come to collect their wine every year. There is no difficulty in selling all the wine that is made, and so it is rather sad that the other vineyards of Auxerre have disappeared under concrete and tarmac.

Irancy

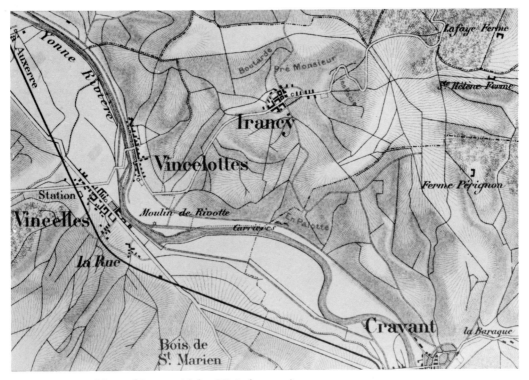

Map of Irancy (*Atlas Vinicole*, 1901)

Irancy is a pretty little village; it nestles on the valley floor, with its vineyards forming an amphitheatre around it. Cherry orchards break up the landscape of vines. There is one long street, lined with old grey stone houses, all with vaulted cellars, some even on two levels, for, in the words of one grower, 'le pays est creux comme un fromage de gruyère' ('The place is hollow like a gruyère cheese'). Irancy is known for its connections with Jacques Germain Soufflot, the architect of the Panthéon and the Hôtel de Ville in Paris. He was born here, and also designed the parish church. His birthplace, the Maison Soufflot, is one of the more imposing houses in the main street.

As elsewhere in the Yonne, the origins of the vineyards were probably Roman, but their growth and development were undoubtedly due to the influence of the monastery of Saint Germain d'Auxerre. In

990 the church of Saint Germain d'Irancy was placed under the tutelage of the monastery in Auxerre, and this contact remained until the Revolution eight centuries later.

Unlike Coulanges-la-Vineuse, which was spared during the Wars of Religion, Irancy was razed to the ground by the Huguenots in February 1568. It is said that all the inhabitants were murdered, except for some women and the *curé*, and so the population of the village did not die out entirely!

By 1824 vines accounted for 355 of the 1198 hectares of the commune. Jullien mentions in particular Palotte (which is, in fact, in the adjoining commune of Cravant), saying that its wine should not be bottled until four years after the vintage. In his opinion Irancy 'produces wines of a fine colour, rich and strong'. He also mentions other forgotten vine-yards, such as Paradis, Bergère, Vaux-Chassés and Cailles.[1] Cyrus Redding, writing in 1832,[2] also praises la Palotte as being among the best wines of the Auxerrois. Certainly by the mid-nineteenth century it had acquired a reputation for longevity.

After the phylloxera crisis the vineyards of Irancy fell into sad decline. Many were never replanted, and even more were abandoned during the First World War, when there was a shortage not only of labour, but also of horses, for these were requisitioned by the army. Instead of Pinot Noir, hybrids proliferated in the vineyards. The revival of Irancy began soon after the Second World War. The hybrids were pulled up and the Pinot Noir regained its former importance. There are now 149 hectares of vines in the commune; the limit has been reached. Although there is still land that could be planted, it is too steep and would be impractical to cultivate.

The reputation of Irancy is now such that it has its own appellation. The decree was passed by the INAO in 1977; hitherto the wine was labelled Bourgogne Rouge, with the concession of Irancy being allowed a mention on the label. The Syndicat de la Défense de l'Appellation, which was created in 1970, was the moving force in the acquisition of the appellation. This body now plays an important organizational role in the control of new plantings and the *labellisation* tastings to which the appellation is subject. The Syndicat des Viticulteurs, whose mem-bership is similar, organizes the various wine festivals of the year, such as La Fête du Sauvignon and La Fête de la Vigne, and arranges any

[1] Op. cit.
[2] *A History and Description of Modern Wines.*

promotional activities for the vineyard.

And so today the main grape variety for Irancy is Pinot Noir – the grape of all fine red burgundy. Its name comes from the small compact bunches, shaped like a pine-cone. It ripens early (an advantage in a northern climate), but also has an early bud-break and so may be susceptible to spring frosts. However it thrives in, and gives the best results in, a cooler climate. It is fairly resistant to diseases, but needs careful treatment in the vineyards to prevent botrytis.

As well as Pinot Noir, small quantities of César or Romain are found in Irancy. The Roman origins of the César grape have already been discussed. It is added to some Irancy to give greater colour, body and tannin, and normally would not be vinified on its own. However, there are exceptions to every rule, as Michel Esclavy of Saint Bris has proved in this instance. Generally the César needs a good exposure to ripen and is more susceptible to frost than Pinot Noir. It also suffers badly from *coulure*.

The Tressot (or Tresseau) is also permitted in the Yonne, but it has virtually disappeared. It did not adapt to being grafted, and although it is quite alcoholic, it tends to lack body. Some Gamay, and a negligible amount of Aligoté used by the SICAVA, are also found.

The vineyards of Irancy encircle the village, with a south and south-west aspect, so that they benefit from the maximum amount of sunshine. The enormous amphitheatre has its own special micro-climate, in that it is warmer than Coulanges and there is much less danger of frost than in Chablis. As in the other vineyards of the Auxerrois, frost protection is generally financially unviable, except in very susceptible areas. The vineyards nearest the Yonne and closest to the valley floor are the most frost-prone. Léon Bienvenu has one hectare protected by fuel heaters; he has used them twice in ten years in this particular vineyard, which suffered badly from frost before he bought it. Hail is considered to be more of a problem than frost, for the damage caused by a May hail-storm can be devastating.

The soil is kimmeridgian, with the same oyster fossils that contribute to the character of Chablis. In view of the calcareous content of the soil, the main graft is the 41B. Experiments are being carried out with other types, for the 41B delays the ripening of the grapes, which is a disadvantage in a northern climate. The pruning is the *taille guyot* method. Otherwise, the problems and treatments in the vineyards do not differ from those which obtain elsewhere in the Yonne.

As well as red wine, Irancy makes rosé. It was first produced in the

1930s and by 1945, with the new fashion for pink wine, accounted for eighty per cent of the production of Irancy. However, since 1960 there has been a definite reversal, with red wine accounting for eighty per cent and rosé merely twenty per cent of the production of the village. As from the 1981 vintage the rosé lost the right to the appellation of Irancy and became simple Bourgogne Rosé.

It is to red wine that Irancy really owes its reputation. There are two styles of Irancy, depending on the use of the César grape. Gabriel Delaloge, for instance, specifically produces two different wines: a lighter, more elegant Irancy, made from pure Pinot Noir, which is ready to drink earlier than his other wine, which has ten, if not twenty, per cent César and accordingly more body and backbone. The César is fermented together with the Pinot Noir in this instance. Other growers, such as André Delaloge, do not have any César, as they dislike the element of hardness that it gives to the wine. The stalks are not removed, so as to give the wine more of the body and backbone mentioned above. This is one of the significant changes that the mechanical harvester would bring about. This, however, is an innovation which has not yet reached the slopes of Irancy.

Some growers, such as Gabriel Delaloge and his cousin André, still have their original stone fermentation tanks. Whereas wood was used in the Côte d'Or before the introduction of cement, in the Yonne, and in particular in Irancy, stone was the norm.

Vinification methods are classic: the grapes are not destalked; the fermentation temperature is controlled; after the malolactic fermentation has occurred the wine is matured in oak or chestnut barrels for twelve to eighteen months, depending on the character of the vintage. There seems to be little difference in the respective merits of chestnut and oak, nor are there any partisans of new oak in Irancy. The rosé is vinified like white wine, after spending one to two days on the skins.

Ironically, the best known vineyard is Palotte, which covers about seven hectares in the adjoining commune of Cravant. Although it is an extension of the vineyards of Irancy, it is only entitled to the appellation of Bourgogne Rouge. This small vineyard is split between fifteen owners. There are other vineyards within Irancy that are less well-known and would merit as fine a reputation.

There are also vineyards in the commune of Vincelottes, on the Yonne, that are also a continuation of the slopes of Irancy. Again, they have the appellation of Bourgogne Rouge and are mostly cultivated by the growers of Irancy. Vincelottes was one of the old river ports which were used to send wine to Paris.

The largest of the peripheral vineyards is Domaine de Pérignon, a thirty-four hectare estate, planted with Pinot Noir (thirty hectares) and Gamay (four hectares), that produces Passe Tout Grains. It was originally planted by some Algerian *pieds noirs*[1] some fifteen years ago, in the hope that the site would merit the appellation of Irancy. This hope was not realized, and the estate is now run from Beaune by the company of Chauvenet.

The average enterprise is a small family concern, with a father and son cultivating a few hectares of vines. Often they have cherry-trees as well, and even some cereal crops, but vines predominate. Generally there is a move towards larger holdings, as some families will disappear in cases where there are no heirs. Today there are twenty-five growers, nearly all of whom bottle some, if not all, their wine. However, many sell a larger proportion of their production to the *négociants* of Chablis. Simmonet Febvre, in particular, are important purchasers of Irancy. This dependence on the *négoce* has caused commercial problems in Irancy, not unlike those of Chablis. Sales stagnated when the *négociants*, after making substantial purchases of the large 1979 vintage, failed to continue their commercial support.

Normally about sixty per cent of an average crop would be bought by the *négoce*; the remaining forty per cent would be sold direct by the growers: to private individuals, to restaurants (both in the locality and in Paris) and – a very little – on the export market. However, the trend is for the growers to sell more wine themselves and thus avoid the price fluctuations and other problems that they feel are caused by the *négoce*. This has had the beneficial effect of an improvement in vinification methods and a more responsible attitude towards the quality of their wine, now that it is sold under their own names.

The great vintage of Irancy was 1947; the summer was hot, there was no rain, and the vintage began two weeks early, on 15 September. The wine reached at least 14° alcohol level. André Delaloge remembers 1921 as another great year. The star year of the last century was 1893, although it is said that 1947 was even better. Since then 1949, 1955, 1959, 1962, 1964, 1966, 1976 and 1978 have all produced notable wines.

The quality of the vintage tends to follow that of Chablis, but this is not an infallible guide, for there is the simple difference between red and white wine. Certainly it is not necessarily the same as that of the

[1] Expatriate French who returned to France from Algeria in the early 1960s.

Côte d'Or, for the two regions are separated by the hills of the Morvan. The years 1980 and 1981 were both more successful in Irancy than in Beaune. Irancy is a wine that will age; it needs at least five years before it is drunk and, with a fine vintage, can remain on its plateau for at least twenty years. I am told that the 1947 is still drinking well in 1982.

The principal growers of Irancy are Léon Bienvenu, Bernard Cantin, André Delaloge, Gabriel Delaloge and Jean Renaud.

Léon Bienvenu

Léon Bienvenu is president of the growers' *syndicat* in Irancy. He lives up to his name as a very hospitable, cheerful man, with a rosy-cheeked, smiling face under his checked beret. His family, as growers in Irancy, date back to 1700. With his son Serge he cultivates 9.5 hectares of vines, mainly Pinot Noir, but he also owns 70 ares of César and a hectare of Gamay à Jus Blanc for Passe Tout Grains. He owns a small parcel of Palotte and makes some rosé as well as the traditional red Irancy. His wine has plenty of body and fruit. His 1979, tasted in December 1981, was very concentrated and needed a much greater bottle age. A comparison of his 1980 Irancy and 1980 Palotte was interesting; both had just been bottled in May 1982. The Palotte (which includes some César) was very closed, with a great deal of potential, whereas the Irancy was slightly softer, with more obvious fruit. However, it was with a 1976 Irancy that his wine really excelled. In December 1981 it was still very young, with plenty of rich Pinot Noir fruit, and drank very well with a Chablis speciality, 'Boudin Blanc au Ratafia' (a kind of white sausage cooked in ratafia).

Bernard Cantin

Bernard Cantin is the Mayor of Irancy. His family have been growers for generations and, together with his father, he owns 8.5 hectares of vines, including nearly a hectare of Palotte. He also has thirty hectares of farmland for grain, as well as a few cherry-trees. We compared his 1979 Palotte with his 1979 Irancy. As with Léon Bienvenu's wine, the Palotte had more body and tannin. Vinification methods are identical; the difference comes from the soil and the addition of a small amount of César.

André Delaloge

Since André Delaloge (a cousin of Gabriel Delaloge; see below) is now retired, and his son Roger runs the family holding, he had time to

Léon Bienvenu from Irancy lives up to his name, with his friendly welcome

reminisce about the old days. He remembers how hard the work in the vines was before the arrival of the tractor and how the renaissance of the vineyards of Irancy gradually occurred. His vaulted cellars, which are very typical of the region, date back to 1662; he still has the old stone fermentation vat. He has just over six hectares of Pinot Noir, with no César, and so his style of Irancy is perhaps lighter than some others, but with an attractive fruitiness.

Gabriel Delaloge

Gabriel Delaloge's family (which he traces back to 1610) bore the name De Laloge, and had noble aspirations, until the French Revolution. It then became politic to discard evidence of the noble connection. Delaloge is another of the great characters of Irancy. He was president of the growers' *syndicat* for nearly thirty years and is still very much involved in everything that is happening in the village. He was very happy to spend an afternoon telling me all about it. He has five hectares of vines, including forty ares of César, and consequently makes two styles of Irancy: without and with César. His 1979 pure Pinot Noir, tasted in December 1981, was very elegant and contained some tannin which would keep it young for another four or five years.

Jean Renaud

Jean Renaud is a serious *viticulteur*, as befits the president of the Syndicat de la Défense de l'Appellation. He began with two hectares of vines inherited from his parents, together with half a hectare of cherry-trees. He now has eight hectares: six of Pinot Noir and two of Gamay, both Gamay à Jus Blanc (for Passe Tout Grains) and Gamay Teinturier (for everyday *vin ordinaire*). He and his son between them have fifteen ares of César at Palotte, but no César in Irancy, and so his Irancy is made from pure Pinot Noir, with fifteen to eighteen months of oak ageing. His Palotte, with the addition of the César, has more body. Most of his wine is sold from the cellar door; he has a good local clientèle and a small export market.

The other growers in Irancy are as follows:

Jack Bourguignat	René Charriat
Edmond Berthelot	Germain Darles
Gilbert Cottin	Michel and Marcel Garlan
Robert and Jean-Pierre Colinot	François Givaudin

Lucien Joudelat
André Melou
Meslin et Fils
Yves Navarre
Jean Podor

Patrick Podor
Daniel Quintard
Pierre Rey
Richoux et Fils
Cyprien and Daniel Vincent

Joigny

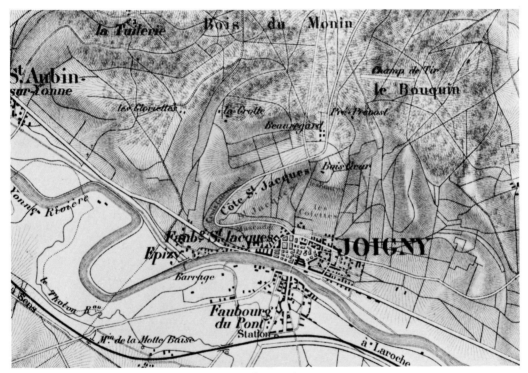

Map of Joigny (*Atlas Vinicole*, 1901)

Once there were vineyards all along the valley of the Yonne, from Migennes, past Joigny, Saint Julien-du-Sault and Villeneuve-sur-Yonne, as far as Sens. Although Sens was important as a river port, its wines were never highly rated. Jullien only mentions them in passing and Guyot not at all. Today all these vineyards have disappeared without trace, except for one small vineyard on the Côte Saint Jacques at Joigny. The history of the vineyards of Joigny is not dissimilar to that of the other vineyards of the Yonne. It owes its significance to its position, and in particular to its proximity to the river, for Joigny was one of the main ports from which wine was sent to Paris. It suffered the decline common to other areas, but at one time enjoyed a certain reputation.

In the seventeenth century Sieur Leboeuf, captain of the civilian militia of Joigny, was a fervent enthusiast for the wines of the Côte Saint Jacques, for he believed that 'it is a truculent wine that makes those who love it father male children'.

Jullien (1822) classifies the Côte Saint Jacques in his third category and the other vineyards of Joigny in fourth place. He describes them as 'light wines, delicate, lively and very pleasant, but with the disadvantage of going straight to your head'.[1]

Later in the century Guyot is not so flattering: 'The wines of Joigny are bourgeois wines; three-quarters of those from the rest of the area are common wines.'[2] He explains how the vineyards of Côte Saint Jacques and the other vineyards of Joigny were once planted with Pinot Noir, Blanc and Gris, with a little Épicier and Plant du Roi (an old name for the Côt or Malbec), but that by the second half of the nineteenth century the demand for cheap wine was such that there was hardly any Pinot left in the vineyards. By then they were mostly planted with Verrot, Plant du Roi and other varieties (such as Mélier, Gois and Épicier) that would produce wine in quantity to satisfy the Parisian market. But this vital outlet could not last for ever. The railways bringing the cheap wines from the Midi caused a sharp fall in the demands from the capital, and the effects of phylloxera and rural depopulation completed the decline of the vineyards of Joigny.

Before the phylloxera crisis there were seven hundred hectares of vines in the commune of Joigny; the Côte Saint Jacques covered an entire hillside, right down to the river bank, with forty-nine hectares of vines overlooking the Yonne. Amusingly, the shape of the hill is such that, with its reflection in the river, the Côte Saint Jacques looks like a long-necked wine bottle. Today there are just four hectares of vines, and even these would have disappeared entirely if it had not been for the enthusiasm of one man, Jacques Vignot. There have always been vines on Vignot's family's land; he has kept and expanded the vineyard a little as he enjoys it. His main business lies in a nursery for poplar-trees, and he also has some farmland.

[1] Op. cit.
[2] Op. cit.

Joigny has no specific appellation of its own; its wine has the appellation Bourgogne, and there is the right to add the name Côte Saint Jacques. The area was defined by the INAO in 1975 and in theory it would be possible to plant another seven hectares of vines. In practice, however, the land is more valuable for building.

The vineyards face south, at an altitude of 110 and 120 metres. The soil is a clay and calcareous mixture, and so the vines are grafted onto 41B rootstock, the variety best able to resist chlorosis in a very chalky soil. The pruning is the *guyot* system, and the vines are planted in rows of 1.1 metres, with a metre between rows. Originally Monsieur Vignot only had Pinot Gris, to make the *vin gris*, or light rosé, for which Joigny was traditionally known when rosé was fashionable earlier in the century; but, with the greater demand for red wine, he planted some Pinot Noir and began making red wine in about 1979. In contrast to Irancy and Coulanges-la-Vineuse, there was never any César in the vineyards of Joigny, only a little Tressot.

Frost rarely causes any damage; the last time the vines suffered from spring frost was in 1977, when the vegetation was particularly advanced. More often the problem is one of uncertain weather. The vines are treated in the same way as elsewhere in the Yonne, with the same precautions against rot and mildew. The average yield is about fifty hectolitres per hectare.

Jacques Vignot follows the traditional methods of vinification. The *vin gris* is made from Pinot Gris (with its lightly coloured skin), although no mention of this may be made on the label. The juice is left on the skins for a few hours, depending on the condition of the grapes; then a standard white wine vinification is carried out. The fermentation lasts for eight to ten days. Traditionally, the *vin gris* of Joigny was considered to be a wine that was capable of considerable longevity. The years 1947, 1949 and 1959 have the reputation of great vintages. Personally, I preferred the fresh fruitiness of the 1981 to the over-mature flavour of the 1975.

Red wine is rather a new venture for Vignot. He follows traditional methods: his wine is aged in wood, both old and new, for twelve to eighteen months before bottling. His barrels come from a *tonnelier* at Sens. Although he aims to make a *vin de garde*, at present the style is lighter than that of the wines of the Auxerrois, with less acidity than those of Coulanges and less tannin than those of Irancy. The 1981 that I tasted from barrel in May 1982 was still very young and closed, and difficult to assess.

Sadly, Vignot's enthusiasm for his vines is shared only by his nephew, Serge Lepage. No one else in Joigny shows any inclination to revive a disappearing tradition. The wines are really only a local curiosity and are sold to local restaurants and private individuals. However, it would be sad if they were to disappear completely.

Although the vines of the Côte Saint Jacques are the only vines in the area which are entitled to *appellation contrôlée* status, there are small pockets of vines from which the growers make table wine purely for home consumption. In the village of Champvallon, a few miles from Joigny, there is an old wine press that used to belong to the local château and is still maintained in regular use to press the hotch-potch of grapes grown in the village.

The old press at Champvallon, still in regular use

Saint Bris-le-Vineux

Of the four communes of the Auxerrois, Saint Bris-le-Vineux is the largest. It takes its name from a Christian martyr, Saint Prix, whose name was changed to Saint Brix over the centuries. The addition of le Vineux apparently occurred after the Revolution.

There are early references to vines in the commune. A modern authority, Roger Dion, mentions that in 1180 'there was at Saint Bris a vineyard of the same size as the one the king owned at Triel in Paris. Its owner estimated the production at a hundred muids in both good and bad years.'[1]

The Templar monks, who were an important force in the area, did much to develop the vineyards of Saint Bris, which were well established by the fourteenth century. In a letter written in 1394 Charles VI says that a grower in Saint Bris 'killed in a fit of anger a workman who had dared to mix *treceaux* and other grapes with *pinot*'. This is probably the earliest reference to the Pinot grape variety.

Saint Bris suffered during the upheavals of the Hundred Years War. In 1358 it was burnt down by the English, who already held Auxerre, and nine years later the troops of the Black Prince pillaged it again. And so fortifications were built at the end of the fourteenth century which survived until the mid-eighteenth. There is also a vast network of cellars under the town which were often used as a place of refuge by the inhabitants of the surrounding countryside during attacks. Most date back to the twelfth century; some are even earlier, and were designed to withstand a long siege. The cellars of the Bersan family even have an old bread oven. Today they are ideal for the storage of wine, but not so practical for its handling and treatment.

As elsewhere in the Yonne during the last century, inferior, high-yielding grape varieties made their appearance, such as Plant du Roi, Lombard, Epicier, Damery and so on. From the lack of mention of the wines of Saint Bris by the authorities of the nineteenth century, it would seem that its wines were not worthy of much attention. Jullien places the reds in his fourth category and the white in second place, but other authorities, such as Cavoleau and Guyot, remain silent about them.

The introduction of *appellation contrôlée* regulations in the 1930s had a significant effect on the quality of the wines of Saint Bris. Instead of the

---

[1] *Histoire de la Vigne et du Vin en France des Origines au XIX Siècle.*

hotch-potch of grape varieties that were usually vinified all together, they were separated, and noble varieties were planted once again. Today Saint Bris is known for its Sauvignon, but also makes Chardonnay, Pinot Noir, Gamay, Aligoté, Sacy and even a little César; in other words, it produces a vinous pot pourri: Bourgogne Rouge and Blanc, Bourgogne Grand Ordinaire and Passe Tout Grains, Bourgogne Aligoté and even Crémant de Bourgogne. It is only the Sauvignon that possesses any regional individuality, with the classification of VDQS for Sauvignon de Saint Bris. For the other *appellation contrôlée* wines there is an unofficial toleration of the term, but no legitimate basis for the mention on the label of Coteaux de Saint Bris.

The origins of the Sauvignon grape variety in the region are uncertain. It is not traditionally a Burgundian grape, which is why the wine made from it is not accorded an appellation. In all probability it came to the area from Sancerre, which is only about eighty miles away. However, there are invoices in existence that show that in 1860 Sauvignon vines were sold from the Yonne to Sancerre. Before the introduction of controlling regulations, and even before the onset of phylloxera, it was one of the hotch-potch of grapes used in the region, but, with the introduction of *appellation contrôlée* it was separated from the communal brew and was widely planted in the post-war years. In 1974 it was recognized as a Vin Délimité de Qualité Supérieure and by 1981 there were sixty-three hectares of Sauvignon. Most growers have a small parcel of it, but they do not rank it with their important wines. Although it is a wine that has acquired a certain reputation in Britain, it is difficult to sell, in that it falls between the expensive quality of Sancerre and the cheap high yields of Touraine, so that it can compete with neither. Another disadvantage is that it cannot be used by the SICAVA for Crémant de Bourgogne, which is another factor in its decline in popularity. Mostly it is sold locally, or in Paris, or to the Chablis *négociants* for the export market. No more is being planted.

Perhaps the most traditional white grape of Saint Bris is the Aligoté. It is said that the Aligoté of Saint Bris is rivalled only by the Aligoté of Pernand Vergelesses in the Côte d'Or, and that it surpasses all others. Certainly my first taste of an Aligoté from Saint Bris (with Jean-François Bersan) was a revelation. Any preconceived ideas about a thin green acidic wine, without any fruit, went to the wind; this was quite different. True, the acidity was there, but there was an underlying honied character on both the nose and the palate. One of the reasons for its quality is that, in the Yonne, Aligoté is grown on well-favoured sites, whereas further south it is planted on inferior hillsides. Unlike Sauvignon, Aligoté, if well made, will improve in bottle, whereas Sauvignon should generally be drunk in early youth. Sadly the appellation regulations prevent the naming of the exact origins of Bourgogne Aligoté, and so it is not always possible to locate an Aligoté from Saint Bris.

The grape variety Sacy takes its name from the village of the same name to the east of Nitry, where the writer Restif de la Bretonne spent his childhood, memories of which are described in *La Vie de Mon Père*. Sacy has also been called Essert, from the name of an adjoining village. It is a very fertile grape variety, with high yields, and, with its high acidity, is above all a grape for Crémant de Bourgogne. Most of the growers send their production to the SICAVA, but some also use it for Bourgogne Grand Ordinaire.

Chardonnay is the other significant white grape variety. Outside Chablis it makes simple Bourgogne Blanc, and is also a permitted variety for Crémant de Bourgogne.

Saint Bris has never been renowned for its red wines. However, about fifteen years ago there was a move to increase the production of red wine in the area when white wine sales were stagnating, and more Pinot Noir and Gamay were planted. The Pinot Noir makes Bourgogne Rouge and Gamay is used with it for Passe Tout Grains and also Bourgogne Grand Ordinaire. Some people also make rosé.

The César was grown all over the Auxerrois before the phylloxera crisis. Today it is found mainly in Irancy but a very little is also grown in Saint Bris. Traditionally, it is considered essential to temper it with Pinot Noir, for, alone, it would normally be too coarse and quite undrinkable. However, this idea has been disproved by Michel Esclavy, who, in 1976, made a wine purely from César as an experiment, as he was convinced of the grape's quality. The result, which I tasted in December 1981, has a great deal of tannin, fruit and concentration, with a very long finish, and a certain Italian quality, not altogether unlike a wine from Piedmont. It must be said, however, that the 1976 vintage was very ripe and exceptional; and it is doubtful whether the César could produce such drinkable results in less favourable years. In any case, the grape is particularly susceptible to *coulure* at the flowering, and so the crop is likely to be minimal in years of inclement weather. The year 1893, one of the great hot vintages of the last century, produced a superlative César.

The mixture of vines at Saint Bris is the outcome partly of history and partly of the influence of geological factors and soil variations. There is both portlandian and kimmeridgian soil, and therefore a calcareous and clay mixture. The altitude of the vineyards varies between 150 and 400 metres. The best vineyards face south-west and south-east. They are affected by frost, but never to the same extent as those in Chablis. As Saint Bris is some distance from the River Yonne, the atmosphere is less humid than in Chablis, where the Serein runs at the foot of the *grands crus* vineyards. In any case, protection against frost would be economically unviable, as elsewhere in the region. Some grape varieties, such as Sacy and Sauvignon, are more resistant to frost than others, and the areas that are particularly prone to frost, such as the lower slopes, remain unplanted. However, the vineyards of Saint Bris did suffer from frost in 1981, when an average yield of only fifteen hectolitres per hectare was obtained, as opposed to the usual forty-five to fifty.

Treatments in the vineyards do not vary particularly from grape variety to grape variety, nor differ from those adopted elsewhere in the region. Some varieties are more susceptible to one malady or another. The Aligoté is quite fragile and suffers from *coulure* (like the César); Sacy is prone to *pourriture grise*. Apart from Chardonnay, which is pruned in the same way as in Chablis, the *taille guyot* (or single *guyot*) is used, and the rootstocks are the same as in Chablis: the 41B and SO4.

Vinification methods are generally traditional and unaffected by trends towards modernization. In contrast to the practice at Irancy, the Pinot Noir is usually destalked before fermentation, so that the wine is lighter and less tannic. It usually spends six to eight days on the skins and is generally kept in wood for twelve months. New oak barrels are an uncommon sight.

Some people heat their cellars, to ensure that the malolactic fermentation occurs without too much delay. Others are content to let nature take its course, and also let the tartrates precipitate naturally in the winter cold. Of the white wines, only Chardonnay will spend any time in wood; the others are all bottled as soon as the malolactic fermentation has occurred.

Saint Bris is an area of small growers and small family holdings, averaging about ten hectares. As in Chablis, most of the growers originally owned a couple of horses, two or three cows and some farmland, in addition to their vines. The example of Robert Defrance is fairly typical. In 1955 he had two horses and two cows; in 1959 he bought a tractor and replaced the two horses with three cows. Later, in 1965, he began to bottle his wine himself, rather than selling it all to the *négoce*, and therefore gave up the cows and the farmland and modernized his equipment.

Cherry-trees were also once an important part of the rural economy of Saint Bris, but now, sadly, they are disappearing as they are no longer remunerative. Four years may seem a long time to wait for a vine to produce grapes, but it takes ten years for a new orchard to produce cherries. Previously Saint Bris had had the advantage of its proximity to the market of Les Halles in Paris, and the freshly picked cherries could be on sale soon after midnight. Now Les Halles have gone, and the market of Rungis does not open until six in the morning, in time for the arrival of the cheaper cherries from Italy. With the loss of this advantage, many cherry orchards have been converted into vineyards.

It would be impossible to write about Saint Bris without mentioning ratafia. Although ratafia is more commonly associated with Champagne, its home was, in fact, Lower Burgundy. The origins of the word are Latin, being derived from *rata fiat* (which became *ratafié*), meaning a drink taken to celebrate the conclusion of a legal or commercial agreement of some sort. Today many of the growers make a small amount of ratafia for home consumption, and it is quite an honour to be offered some as a *bonne bouche* at the end of a tasting. Ratafia is the combination of marc and grape must; the marc is distilled by a mobile alembic still which usually spends a couple of months at Saint Bris each year. Often the ratafia is left to mature on old lees in small oak barrels, and many people have their own special recipes, which are closely guarded secrets.

Saint Bris always has been and always will be a wine-producing community. Several question-marks, however, hang over its future.

At the moment there are some fifty growers cultivating some five hundred hectares of vines; but many of these growers have no heirs, and so there are doubts about the future of these vineyards. Moreover, for this reason, although there is still land available for planting vines, the vineyard area of the village is unlikely to grow.

As elsewhere in the Yonne, there has been a move away from the *négociants*. More and more people prefer the independence of bottling and selling at least a part of their wine. The reason for this is that although Saint Bris has been less affected by price fluctuations than Chablis, these nevertheless have had an impact on the market and have resulted in a certain disenchantment with the *négoce*. However, most of the wine from this area to be found on the export market still comes from *négociants*, rather than from individual growers.

The appellation status of Saint Bris is ill-defined. There has been a movement among the growers for a more precise appellation, but even the tolerance of Coteaux de Saint Bris on a label is in doubt at the time of writing. Apart from Sauvignon, the wines are part of the vast and anonymous Bourgogne appellations. The vineyard area of the village has also to be defined. At present, provided a wine passes the *labellisation* tasting, it is acceptable as an appellation wine. Where the definition of the vineyards is concerned, local politics come into play. As in Chablis, there are two *syndicats* of growers. The long-established, traditional Syndicat du Vignoble de l'Auxerrois is headed by Michel Esclavy, who has played an important role in the development of the economy of the region, both for wine (with the setting-up of the SICAVA) and for cherry-trees. His widespread activities have caused resentment and jealousy among some of the growers, with the result that there is now a second *syndicat*, headed by Jean-Louis Bersan, whose aim is the promotion of the wines of the Auxerrois. This Syndicat de la Défense des Appellations des Vignobles de l'Auxerrois has a much more broad-minded attitude towards the question of the definition of the vineyards than the older *syndicat*. Some growers, however, belong to both!

The growers in Saint Bris whom I visited are Louis Bersan et Fils, Jean Brocard, Robert Defrance, Michel Esclavy and André Sorin.

Louis Bersan et Fils

Following their father's death in 1980, the company is now run by two brothers, Jean-Louis and Jean-François Bersan. The Bersans are a very long-established family in Saint Bris; the earliest reference to them was in 1450, in a document concerning a wine fraud! Their cellars in the centre of the town date back to the eleventh century; they are a veritable labyrinth of passages, with the remains of a bread oven and an old stone *fouloir*. It is all very picturesque, but highly impractical. Their vineyard holdings are very typical of an average grower in Saint Bris, with eight hectares of Pinot Noir (for Bourgogne Rouge), one of Gamay (for Bourgogne Grand Ordinaire and Passe Tout Grains), five of Aligoté, two-and-a-half of Sacy (for Bourgogne Grand Ordinaire and Cremant de Bourgogne), thirty acres of Melon de Bourgogne, one hectare of Chardonnay (for Bourgogne Blanc) and three hectares of Sauvignon. Like some of the other growers in Saint Bris, they also have a small interest in Chablis, with two hectares planted at Préhy in 1981. They are gradually increasing their production, aiming for a total holding of twenty-five hectares. In addition to making wine, they act as *courtiers* for some of the *négociants* of Chablis and the Côte d'Or. Most of their wine is sold in bottle on the French market, often to private individuals, and a little is exported.

Their wines are attractive. We tasted a honied Aligoté and a fresh, perfumed Sauvignon. The Pinot Noir, which is aged in wood for a few months, was rather light, with quite high acidity, indicating that the soil of Saint Bris is not really suitable for Pinot Noir. Our tasting concluded with a glass of ratafia – very warming on a December morning.

Jean Brocard

Jean Brocard is one of the more *avant garde* growers of Saint Bris. He is a young man, who has built up his own vineyards over the past ten years, beginning in 1973 with one hectare that belonged to his father-in-law. He now has a couple of hectares of Aligoté and Pinot Noir in Saint Bris, but has really concentrated his activities in Chablis – or, rather, on the edge of the appellation at Préhy, where he now has eighteen hectares. Sauvignon does not interest him, as it is not a true Burgundian grape variety and cannot compete with Sancerre.

Brocard was the first grower in the Auxerrois to use a mechanical harvester, which he finds gives good results, provided that care is taken to avoid oxidation. Altogether he gives the impression of being a very serious wine-maker. His cellars are modern and he uses classic methods. His red wine spends a year in wood.

Robert Defrance

Robert Defrance, whose family vineyards go back three generations, cultivates eleven hectares with his son Philippe. Aligoté predominates (with four hectares), and he has 2.5 hectares of Sauvignon, one of Sacy and 2.5 of Pinot Noir. He has also just planted a hectare of Chardonnay that will come into production in 1985. Since 1967 Defrance has sold all his wine in bottle. His twelfth-century vaulted cellars contain a statue of Saint Vincent, the patron saint of the wine-maker.

Defrance believes strongly in the importance of hygiene in wine-making and in the need for a carefully controlled fermentation. No oak is used; his Pinot Noir is bottled fifteen months after the vintage and the white as soon as the malolactic fermentation is over.

My tasting notes include references to a very perfumed Sauvignon (quite full and with plenty of flavour), a lightly fruity Aligoté and a Pinot Noir which had an elegant fruitiness, but also the typical acidity of Saint Bris wines.

Michel Esclavy

Michel Esclavy is a man of considerable responsibilities in the area. It is hardly an exaggeration to say that he is 'President de Tout', for his activities encompass the INAO, the SICAVA, the Confrérie des Trois Ceps and the wine committees of the commune, the *département* and the region. A man of considerable energy and determination, he has devoted much of his time to the region.

His own vineyards cover some fifteen hectares, with six hectares of Pinot Noir, a little Gamay for home consumption, six hectares of Aligoté, 1.2 of Sauvignon, a couple of Sacy (which goes to the SICAVA) and a tiny plot of twenty-five ares of César. His methods are traditional, but he favours neutral vats, rather than oak barrels, as he aims to concentrate the fruit and flavour of each grape variety. He makes red and rosé wine from his Pinot Noir; the red was not unattractive – as always in this region, very light, but with an attractive fruitiness – and his Sauvignon was deliciously perfumed. Our tasting finished with his unique César, followed by the most deliciously rich ratafia.

André Sorin

André Sorin's grandfather, Andry, began the family business. He now owns thirteen hectares and rents four, broken down into two hectares of Sacy, five of Aligoté (which he is increasing), 2.3 of Sauvignon and 7.7 of Pinot Noir. He plans to plant some Chardonnay, but is not tempted by Chablis, as only the less favourable land is available now.

Sorin's establishment is on the periphery of the town, and his new cellars are much more functional than the traditional cellars of the town centre. His parcel of Pinot Noir is at Vincelottes, a continuation of the hills of Irancy. It was light and fruity – a recognizable Pinot Noir, but with little body. It might age for four or five years, but no more. Sorin considers his Aligoté to be his best wine, and I would not disagree; it was delightfully honied, with fruit and enough, but not too much, acidity. He is a serious wine-maker, with a sense of humour and a quiet and justified confidence in his wines. Eighty per cent of his production is sold locally; the other twenty per cent goes to Belgium – not coincidentally, as he happens to be married to a Belgian.

The other important growers in Saint Bris are as follows:

Yvon Daudier	Serge Goisot
Hugues Goisot	Jean Guimiot

Maurice Jouby
Jacques Mazeau
Guy Persenot
William Pinon
Maurice Renard

Claude Séguin
Michel Sorin
Jean-Paul Tabit
Claude Verret (GAEC du Parc)

Tonnerre and Epineuil

The wines of Tonnerre were first mentioned in a charter of the tenth century. However, it was the ecclesiastical influence during the Middle Ages that was vital to their development. There were vines attached to the collegial church of Saint Michel, and the hospital of Tonnerre, a religious foundation of 1293, was noted as an important vineyard owner.

These wines found early favour with the English; Courtepee records in 1777 that after the Battle of Poitiers in 1356 'the English, who were masters of the countryside, burnt Châtillons and pillaged Tonnerre, where the good wine kept them for five days, without them being able to take the château, which was defended by Baudoin Denckin, captain of the crossbow men'.[1] English appreciation of the wines of Tonnerre lasted, for in the eighteenth century the Chevalier d'Eon, a French diplomat at the court of Louis XV, who resided in London, noted the English enjoyment of the wines of Tonnerre in his correspondence.

Jullien ranks the red wines of Tonnerre alongside those of Auxerre and the whites as approaching Meursault in quality. The adjoining vineyards of Epineuil he places in second rank; they are different from Tonnerre, 'delicats et très spiritueux'. He also mentions 'des vins d'une couleur très pâle que l'on nomme vins gris'.[2] Guyot is slightly less flattering about the white wines of Tonnerre; for him Les Côtes de Vaumorillons and Les Grisées rival Chablis rather than Meursault. He says that the reds are reputed to age for fifty years. He also describes a sparkling wine that has been made in Tonnerre since 1826 as being 'too heavy and not having the finesse and distinction of the fine wines of Champagne'[3]. It was, however, made by the Champagne method, and more from Pinot Noir than from white grapes.

[1] Op. cit.
[2] Op. cit.
[3] Op. cit.

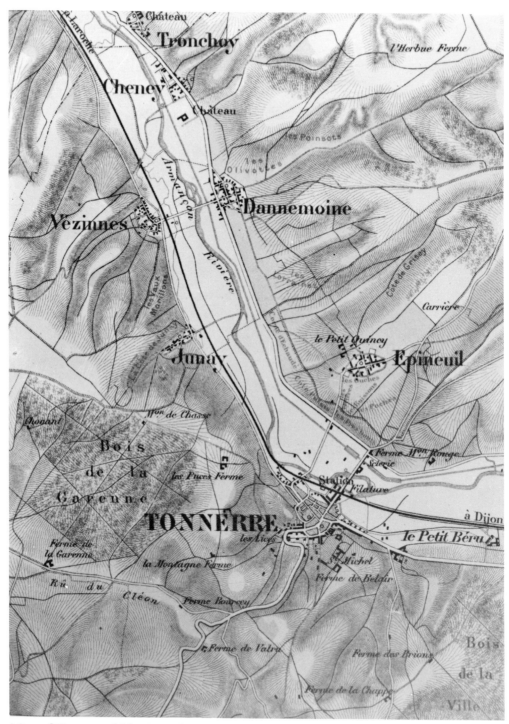

Map of Tonnerre (*Atlas Vinicole*, 1901)

In the nineteenth century the main vineyards were along the valley of the Armançon; the grape varieties were Pinot Noir, Tressot, Romain, Gamay and other now almost forgotten varieties, like Lombard and Plant du Roi and, for whites, Morillon. Already in the nineteenth century Guyot was referring to the scarcity of labour and the problems of maintaining the vineyards; phylloxera virtually administered the coup de grâce. Today all that remains of these once-renowned vineyards are those of Epineuil, and even they might have disappeared had it not been for the one-time Mayor of Epineuil, André Durand.

The name Epineuil is of Latin origin, from *spinoleum* (*épines*, or thistles). In other words, it is a place covered with thistles. Although there was a local lay landowner, the vineyards originally depended mainly upon two religious communities, both of which established houses in Epineuil: the Petit Môlesme (from the Abbey of Môlesme) and the Petit Quincy (an offshoot of the Abbey of Quincy). The latter building still stands. Apparently it contains a beautiful cellar, with an old wine press; but, as the guidebook would say, no visitors are allowed, for it is owned by a reclusive old lady in her eighties.

In 1855 there were 700 inhabitants in the village of Epineuil, with 500 hectares of land under cultivation, of which vines accounted for 305. Most families had a few ares of vines, and there were a few who had more than an hectare. Then came the scourges of *oidium* and phylloxera, and competition from wines from Algeria at the beginning of the century caused a further decline. Of the eighty growers of the village who were mobilized during the First World War, twenty-five were killed; the women were left to run the vineyards as best they could, but many were unable to cope and the land reverted to *friche*, or wasteland. The returning growers were even more discouraged; they were unable to compete with the cheap wines from the south and so, lured by the attractions of Paris, many left the village and the effects of rural depopulation took their toll. By 1955 there were precisely twelve hectares of vines left in what was once a flourishing wine community. These vineyards were planted half with *plantes nobles* and half with hybrids, a further indication of the sorry state of the vineyards of Epineuil.

The situation was saved by André Durand, to whom I have already referred; he succeeded in launching a revival of interest in the wines of Epineuil. Durand arrived in the village in 1938 as a teacher and stayed on after the war. Involving himself in local politics, in 1959 he was elected Mayor of Epineuil. In this capacity he examined the old vineyards, which had reverted to *friche*. He saw that this land could earn the community no money if it were left in such a state, whereas vineyards would be profitable. He was also inspired by the former reputation of Epineuil, which, although it no longer produced the wines to support this renown, was a recognized part of the appellation of Bourgogne, with the right to add the name Epineuil to the label. The exact area has even now not yet been defined; nonetheless, Durand had something concrete on which to build.

He duly enlisted the support of the SAFER; but, even with its help, the project has not been without problems. To begin with, farmers from Tonnerre wanted to claim some of the land, as theirs had been encroached upon for building. Then, two Côte d'Or houses were interested in buying vineyards – but wanted to make the wine in the Côte d'Or. This condition was totally unacceptable, for, if it were implemented, the individuality of Epineuil would have been obliterated.

The main problem, however, was the lack of young people in Epineuil itself who were interested in running a vineyard. Consequently it was necessary to attract interest from outside the area. A few people in the village have bought some ares of vines, but the main growers (the professionals, as Durand calls them) are not natives of Epineuil. The most important of these are Jean-Claude Michaut (who had already worked in Chablis), and, after him, two Champenois (M. Clérot and M. Péan), a Parisian (M. Mathias) and a grower from Châteauneuf-du-Pape (M. Calamel). In 1982 there were twenty-five hectares of vines planted, but not necessarily in production. A further forty hectares were intended for planting, and there were twenty hectares that could be converted into vines. André Durand now feels that the vineyards of Epineuil are on the road to recovering some of their former glory.

There are now four named vineyards in Epineuil: Les Fauconniers (meaning 'falconers'), which faces south-west; Damnots (the name originates from the seigneurial domain of the village), which faces south; Les Froberts (an old name for *grillon*, meaning 'cricket'), which faces west, with a less favourable aspect; and the steep Côtes de Grisey, above the windmill of the same name, which is presumably the same vineyard as the one which was praised by Jullien and Guyot.

Epineuil itself is a pretty little village, with soft-coloured stone houses lining the main street. The vineyards lie on hills to the south and east of the village. Monsieur Durand took me on a tour of them in his van, a bumpy ride along several dirt tracks. The Michaut vineyards are impeccably kept – not a weed to be seen nor a vine out of place. Unfortunately, some of his neighbours are less conscientious; one (who shall remain nameless) has had to replant his vineyard, not once, but twice, as the vines died. The remains of the old vineyards are still visible in the woodland. Durand has a tiny cellar under his house and, as well as a larger vineyard, some vines in his back garden, on the site of the vineyard that once belonged to the monks of Quincy. We tasted a 1978 vin rosé, or *vin gris*, made from Pinot Noir, which would uphold Epineuil's claim to produce the best rosé of France, alongside Marsannay and Tavel. Although red wine predominates in Epineuil today, the village has also been known for its *vin gris*, especially in the period 1920–50, when sales of red wine were less successful.

Today the SAFER will only permit the planting of Pinot Noir on land that is acquired through its mediations. The amateurs, as opposed to the professionals, also have some Gamay for home consumption and Durand is considering a few ares of Pinot Gris as an experiment. Virtually all the hybrids have now disappeared.

The soil in Epineuil has a very high limestone content, and so chlorosis is a considerable problem, which can reduce the yield. To combat this the growers use, for their main grafts, 41B or SO4. Frost damage is rare. The land at the bottom of the valley, which was formerly very frost-prone, has now been built on, and as the rest of the vineyards rarely suffer from frost, no preventative measures are necessary. If they had been necessary, Jean-Claude Michaut says that he would never have considered running a vineyard in Epineuil, as the installation of *chaufferettes* would have been financially impossible. The usual treatments against rot and oidium are carried out and the average yield is about forty hectolitres per hectare.

Jean-Claude Michaut is the most successful of the growers of Epineuil. He is a young man with a strong sense of purpose and an inspiring confidence in his ability to redeem the reputation of Epineuil. He gives the impression of being a talented wine-maker who enjoys what he is doing. His father is a grower at Chichée in the Chablisien. After being trained in wine-making, Michaut worked as a *conseiller viticole* for the Yonne and then for another Chablis grower but he really wanted to create something that was his own, and this is what he has been able to do in Epineuil. In 1977 he bought the last remaining parcel of old vines in the area and in 1978 acquired land from the SAFER. He now has thirteen hectares, of which seven are planted, all in Pinot Noir, and in 1982 four were in production.

At present Michaut makes his wine at Serrigny, a village between Epineuil and Chablis, where he also has some vines, but eventually he intends to build a cellar in Epineuil itself. His vinification methods are classic. He ferments in open-top fibreglass vats, keeping the cap of grape skins submerged. The length of the fermentation varies, depending on the conditions of the vintage. In 1977 the vintage was late and the grapes were cold, and so the fermentation took longer to get going, since Michaut is not equipped to heat his cellars. By contrast, in 1978, with the warmer conditions, the fermentation took only four days. The wine is left in vat to complete its malolactic fermentation. In 1980 this continued until August, but in 1981 it was finished by February. The wine is then aged in old oak vats, for eighteen to twenty-four months, depending on its evolution. Michaut tastes all his wines at least twice every month. For him it is all a question of 'pif de personne', *pif* being a slang word for 'nose'; he is convinced of the importance of closely following the development of his wine.

So far, Michaut is the only grower in Epineuil to market his wines. He sells to local restaurants, private individuals and local retailers, but his production is still very limited. He places the five vintages he has made in descending order of quality: 1978, 1981, 1979, 1980 and 1977. We tasted the 1980, which was the wine he had available at his home in Saint Georges d'Auxerre. It was a light vintage and accordingly a light wine – quite elegant, with good fruit and some acidity. Michaut is convinced that he will be able to make a better wine than those of Coulanges-la-Vineuse or Irancy and that Epineuil will re-establish its former reputation. 'On verra.'

Vézelay

An exhibition was organized at Vézelay in 1971, entitled 'Vingt siècles de Vigne et du Vin à Vézelay'. Twenty centuries is a long time, but this is probably not an exaggeration, for it is likely that the Romans planted vineyards in the area. The discovery in 1689 of a temple dedicated to Bacchus under the old church of Saint Etienne de Vézelay during the building of a new tower would support this argument. Vines feature in the sculptures of the Basilica of Vézelay. The oldest column, which dates from the eleventh century, features Adam and Eve and the serpent with a vine. Eve is tempted not by an apple, but by a bunch of grapes. There are two other interesting pillars: one depicting birds eating grapes; the other, two men, possibly harvesters, also eating grapes.

The vineyards of Vézelay once covered the banks of the River Cure; some belonged to the Abbey of Vézelay and some to two aristocratic landowners, the Duke of Chastellux and the Duke of Burgundy. These vineyards were a small part of the larger area of Avallon, which included the vineyards along the banks of the River Cousin and the hillsides of Annay-la-Côte. They are mentioned by the nineteenth-century authorities. Jullien[1] places Avallon in his third category of red wines; he particularly mentions the Côte d'Annay as being delicate, Côtes du Rouvres as 'full-bodied and solid' and Le Clos at Vézelay as having 'the property of withstanding a sea voyage'. Cavoleau (1827)[2] refers to 'Le Clos de Vézelay'. Cyrus Redding[3] goes into greater detail. He refers to three distinct qualities of red wine, valued at fifty, forty and fifteen francs per hectolitre respectively. The best wines are those of Rouvres, Annay, Monthechérin and Montfaute, Le Clos at Vézelay and Givry (there is a Givry in Lower Burgundy, as well as the better known village of the Côte Chalonnaise). The best of these should be matured in wood for three or four years and then will apparently keep for fifteen to twenty years in bottle.

In 1833 the vineyards of Avallon consisted of some four thousand hectares. However, the principal grape varieties were not those designed to produce wines of quality, but those which produced juice in liberal quantities, such as Gros and Petit Verrot. By 1924 the area had fallen to four hundred hectares, following the effects of phylloxera and rural depopulation. During the Second World War there was a slight revival, in that quantities of hybrid vines were planted to quench the thirst of the Morvan; but these were pulled up in the early 1950s and today there are not even forty hectares of vines in the area.

The vineyards of Vézelay would probably have disappeared entirely if it had not been for a chance quirk of fate. Despite the very marked decline in viticulture in the region, one or two farmers had continued to keep a few vines with which to make their own wine for home consumption. In 1971 one of them, Bernard Basseporte, who was, in fact, on the point of pulling up his vines, entertained a group of journalists who were visiting the region, but asked them not to mention his wine,

[1] Op. cit.
[2] Op. cit.
[3] Op. cit.

as the production was so limited. All those present did as he asked, but one of their number (who was absent on this particular occasion) later asked a colleague for the details. His subsequent article in *La Minute* resulted in Basseporte receiving eight hundred enquiries about his wine. Inspired by this reaction, he began to believe that there was perhaps a future for wine production in Vézelay.

Some ten years later there is a small group of enthusiasts in the villages of Saint Père-sur-Vézelay and Fontette who are trying to revive the vinous traditions of their village, for before the phylloxera crisis there had been some sixty growers in Saint Père cultivating some 350 hectares of vines. New vineyards, which are run by a group of five growers, have been planted with the financial help of the SAFER and the national park of the Morvan.

The SAFER dictated the choice of grape varieties – an interesting choice, for not only are there the traditional Burgundian varieties of Pinot Noir and Chardonnay, but also the Melon de Bourgogne (which, although it was once grown widely in the area, is now more commonly found in Muscadet) and the Auxerrois. The Auxerrois is not normally permitted in the Yonne, but has been especially reinstated in this small area. Its origins are uncertain. It may well have been planted by the monks of Saint Germain d'Auxerre in the Middle Ages and thus acquired its name. Today it is grown in Luxembourg as well as in England, and the Pinot Auxerrois is widely found in Alsace. There is also a little Gamay and Aligoté.

The vines have been planted in unusually wide rows of 2.7 metres, as opposed to the standard 1.35 metres, for experimental reasons, on the advice of the SAFER. A second row could then be added, if necessary. With such wide rows, tractors are easy to manoeuvre and *tracteurs enjambeurs* are not necessary. The vines were planted under plastic, with SO4 rootstock, for the soil is a mixture of clay and limestone. The *taille guyot* pruning method is used for all grape varieties. Frost is much less of a problem than in Chablis, although they did suffer a reduced yield in 1981. Otherwise, the vineyards are much the same as those elsewhere in the Yonne.

Vinification methods are fairly traditional, simple and rustic. The white wines are kept in plastic vats until the malolactic fermentation occurs and the tartrates are left to fall naturally. However, in the case of the Auxerrois the malolactic fermentation is blocked with sulphur, for otherwise the wine would not have enough acidity. It is then filtered and bottled in the spring following the vintage. The red wines are kept in wood for a year before bottling.

Chaptalization is not permitted for a basic *vin de table*, which is what most of these wines are. However, when I visited Vézelay in December 1981 they were optimistic that the Chardonnay and Pinot Noir of that year would pass the *labellisation* tastings and be recognized as Bourgogne *appellation contrôlée* wine, and this has subsequently happened.

Bernard Basseporte is optimistic about the future of the vineyards of Vézelay. He is confident that they will be able to re-establish some kind of recognition for their wines, perhaps as appellation Côtes de Vézelay. The market for the wines is readily available, with the tourist industry of Vézelay, and there is land for replanting. In April 1981 they were given the *droit de plantation* for ten hectares, out of a total of three hundred hectares for the whole of France. There are also some old vineyards that can be pulled up and replanted. Eventually Basseporte hopes that this small group of growers will work together like members of a co-operative, for each of them is primarily a farmer, and viticulture is only a very small part of their activities.

These wines can hardly have any pretensions to greatness, but those tasted on a rather dreary wet December afternoon certainly brightened up the day. Basseporte's cellar is tiny and very rustic; it is full of small oak barrels, and as there is no electricity, we tasted by candlelight. His first vintage of Auxerrois, the 1979, was very fresh, with a slight Alsace pungency and rather high acidity. Then we adjourned to the cellar of a friend, Jean-Gilles Besle, who is an English teacher by profession, but has a hectare of Pinot Noir and Melon de Bourgogne for himself and his three brothers. The afternoon was further enlivened by the antics of a large black labrador answering to the name of Oscar; he had a large black tail designed to cause havoc with glasses in a rather small wine cellar. After more Auxerrois and Melon de Bourgogne, our tasting was concluded with liberal glasses of ratafia. Bernard Basseporte went back to his *charcuterie*, for he had killed a pig that morning, and we drove off uncertainly into the distance.

The only remaining *cabane* (see p. 95) in Chablis,
restored by Jean Pierre Tricon at Domaine de Vauroux

APPENDIX 1

Total Area of Vines in the Yonne (in Hectares)

Year	Appellation Contrôlée	VDQS	Total area, including vin de table
1788			32,168
1849			37,424
1874			43,508
1888			40,060
1909			16,035
1920			12,990
1930			8,950
1940			7,473
1950			6,500
1960			6,000
1970	1,538		3,500
1974	1,569		
1975	1,678		
1976	1,787		
1977	1,975		
1978	2,107		
1979	2,183		
1980	2,258	65	3,300
1981	2,308		

The figures for 1788–1888 are taken (as an approximate indication) from various nineteenth-century authorities, who are sometimes at variance with each other. The later figures were supplied by the tax office in Auxerre.

APPENDIX 2

Areas for Appellations of the Yonne, other than Chablis, in 1981 (in Hectares)

Bourgogne Blanc	29
Bourgogne Rouge and Rosé	189
Bourgogne Grand Ordinaire Blanc	56
Bourgogne Grand Ordinaire Rouge and Rosé	19
Bourgogne Passe Tout Grains	71
Bourgogne Aligoté	152
Crémant de Bourgogne	191
VDQS Sauvignon	63

APPENDIX 3

Chablis: Area in Production (in Hectares)

Year	Grand cru	1er cru	Chablis	Petit Chablis	Total
1942–46	37	200	116	139	492
1947–51	34	225	122	143	524
1952–56	29	225	140	150	544
1966	41	273	304	115	733
1967					
1968					
1969	51	276	342	120	789
1970	59	257	313	128	757
1971					
1972					
1973					
1974	71	260	534	163	1,028
1975	83	306	544	174	1,107
1976	87	333	589	184	1,193
1977	85	410	733	105	1,333
1978	89	437	805	104	1,435
1979	83	439	856	112	1,490
1980	90	463	895	106	1,554
1981	91	474	924	113	1,602
1982	92	477	989	109	1,667

Where there is a fall in the figures, vineyards have been replanted and are not yet in production again.

Chablis was at its lowest ebb just after the Second World War, with under 500 hectares. This rose to over 500 hectares in the mid-1950s, but the big expansion of the vineyard did not take place until the 1970s. Most of these figures were provided by the tax office in Auxerre; the figures for the earlier years were supplied by William Fèvre. Rather surprisingly, the INAO has kept virtually no records of the areas in production. The absolute maximum vineyard area would be 100 (*grand cru*), 750 (*1er cru*), 2,600 (Chablis), 1,800 (Petit Chablis), 5,250 (total).

APPENDIX 4

Authorizations of New Plantings by the INAO, 1967–81 (in Hectares)

Year	Chablis Grand Cru	Chablis 1er Cru	Chablis	Petit Chablis	Total
1967	11·78	7·44	16·27	6·89	42·38
1968	4·32	16·75	25·65	6·94	53·66
1969	1·06	9·58	31·99	9·58	52·21
1970	1·53	9·71	67·25	14·80	93·29
1971	1·58	12·77	53·94	17·72	86·01
1972	3·47	22·26	91·35	25·94	143·02
1973	1·48	19·59	123·73	38·39	183·19
1974	0·36	12·96	69·58	12·03	94·93
1975	2·09	6·56	52·85	8·44	69·94
1976	0·24	2·64	22·57	0·98	26·43
1977	0·50	5·65	33·70	0·43	40·28
1978	1·87	7·60	40·48	0·50	50·45
1979	2·23	29·06	93·29	7·15	131·73
1980	0·86	25·00	120·00	17·00	163·00
1981		9·00	92·00	15·00	116·00
Total 1967–81	33·37	196·57	934·65	181·89	1,346·52
Annual average 1967–81	2·22	13·10	62·31	12·13	89·77

Permission is given in one year for planting in the following year. In other words, 116 hectares of Chablis could be planted in the spring of 1982. This authorization is not necessarily acted upon immediately, but the table illustrates the enormous growth in the vineyards of Chablis during the 1970s.

APPENDIX 5

Yields of Chablis (in Hectolitres)

Year	Grand cru	1er cru	Chablis	Petit Chablis	Total
1942	407	?	7,887	?	?
1943	1,052	6,709	4,964	2,745	15,470
1944	949	6,642	3,238	4,870	15,699
1945	53	241	65	122	481
1946	621	4,477	2,067	3,783	10,948
1947	847	6,332	3,379	4,801	15,359
1948	565	4,718	2,457	3,253	10,993
1949	600	4,023	2,071	2,732	9,426
1950	1,040	8,747	4,562	6,966	21,315
1951	40	3,903	2,739	3,812	10,494
1952	693	5,571	3,305	3,709	13,278
1953	104	2,980	1,441	1,973	6,498
1954	677	7,139	4,243	5,171	17,230
1955	671	7,862	4,795	6,255	19,583
1956	386	3,301	2,238	2,808	8,733
1957	1.3	735	355	600	1,691.3
1958	655	5,472	2,650	2,304	11,081
1959	760	6,838	6,590	3,193	17,381
1960	681	6,088	7,426	2,991	17,186
1961	673	5,359	5,052	2,372	13,456
1962	1,111	9,868	9,393	4,202	24,574
1963	1,389	11,625	11,956	5,044	30,014
1964	1,340	9,723	9,251	3,727	24,041
1965	1,240	8,437	9,295	3,522	22,494
1966	1,896	12,272	13,919	5,209	33,296
1967	1,423	9,691	10,620	3,934	25,668
1968	1,485	7,894	15,752	4,050	29,181
1969	1,890	8,389	9,590	2,458	22,327
1970	?	?	?	?	74,498
1971	356	8,501	11,273	3,753	23,883
1972	2,295	11,233	16,245	5,283	35,056
1973	4,458	19,338	30,249	10,249	64,294
1974	3,115	11,981	29,782	9,300	54,178
1975	3,907	15,591	29,443	9,543	58,484
1976	4,444	16,721	31,934	8,387	61,486
1977	4,147	16,958	26,251	1,856	49,212
1978	3,850	17,731	25,179	2,332	49,092

YIELDS OF CHABLIS (IN HECTOLITRES): CONTINUED

Year	Grand cru	1er cru	Chablis	Petit Chablis	Total
1979	6,124	33,988	66,126	7,989	114,227
1980	5,113	25,491	46,601	5,359	82,564
1981	2,864	15,686	22,749	1,723	43,022
1982	6,075	33,775	69,682	7,375	116,907

It is impossible to give an accurate summary of the yields per hectare without also knowing the area of production, for which, unfortunately, figures are not available in every case. The sources for these figures are various: the Syndicat des Viticulteurs de Chablis, the Station Agronomique d'Auxerre and the Déclarations de récolte.

APPENDIX 6

Prices of Chablis (in Francs, 1976 Value) per Feuillette of 132 litres

	Price in francs at the time	Coefficient	Price in francs (1976)
1920	220	1·17	250
1921	220	1·55	340
1922	220	1·61	350
1923	300	1·35	400
1924	400	1·17	450
1925	450	1·06	480
1926	800	0·82	650
1927	1,200	0·87	1,000
1928	1,500	0·86	1,300
1929	1,800	0·85	1,500
1930	1,000	0·90	900
1931	300	1·00	300
1932	300	1·11	330
1933	300	1·16	350
1934	220	1·22	270
1935	450	1·31	600
1936	450	1·18	530
1937	1,000	0·89	900
1938	550	0·78	430
1939	1,200	0·74	900
1940	1,500	0·59	900
1941	3,000	0·49	1,500
1942	4,000	0·42	1,600
1943	5,000	0·35	1,600
1944	5,000	0·295	1,600
1945	8,000	0·204	1,600
1946	15,000	0·1257	1,800
1947	18,000	0·0834	1,500
1948	18,000	0·0504	900
1949	28,000	0·0448	1,250
1950	18,000	0·0411	750
1951	18,000	0·0336	600
1952	18,000	0·0311	600
1953	20,000	0·0322	650
1954	20,000	0·0324	650

PRICES OF CHABLIS (IN FRANCS, 1976 VALUE) PER FEUILLETTE
OF 132 LITRES: CONTINUED

	Price in francs at the time	Coefficient	Price in francs (1976)
1955	20,000	0·0323	650
1956	20,000	0·0309	600
1957		0·0296	
1958	30,000	0·0262	520
1959	60,000	0·0248	1,500
1960	600	2·41	1,450
1961	600	2·35	1,400
1962	500	2·26	1,150
1963	250	2·17	600
1964	300	2·12	600
1965	300	2·07	600
1966	300	2·02	600
1967	350	1·99	700
1968	450	1·93	900
1969	800	1·80	1,450
1970	600	1·68	1,000
1971	850	1·61	1,370
1972	850	1·52	1,300
1973	900	1·39	1,250
1974	550	1·17	650
1975	900	1·10	1,000
1976	1,400	1·00	1,400
1977	2,000	0·927	1,854
1978	3,500	0·866	3,031
1979	2,000	0·780	1,560
1980	1,200	0·695	834
1981	2,000	0·600	1,800

The third column gives the coefficient used to transform the actual price during the year in question into the equivalent value of the franc in 1976.

*Graph to illustrate the rise and fall of prices of
Chablis (Appendix Six)*

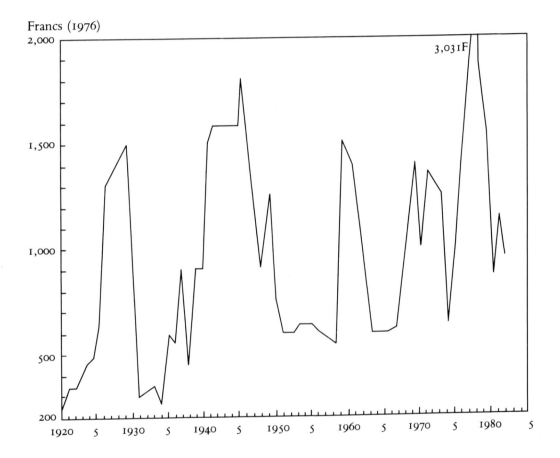

Francs (1976)

APPENDIX 7

Climatic Characteristics of some French Vineyards

	T	A	X	S	R	R A–S
Montpellier	15	259	2,015	1,771	752	313
Orange	14	231	1,754		868	418
Bordeaux	13	236	1,626	1,359	814	366
Tours	11	201	1,189	1,261	689	329
Dijon	11	189	1,175	1,433	739	398
Mâcon	11	192	1,227	1,432	820	445
Chablis	11	180	1,087	1,285	707	367
Reims	10	180	992	1,190	598	322
Colmar	11	194	1,253		519	338

T: average annual temperature
A: number of days with temperature above 10°C
X: total of temperature above 10°C
S: hours of sunshine, April to September
R: total annual rainfall in millimetres
R A–S: total rainfall, April to September, in millimetres

This table is taken from G. J. Gilbank, *Les Vignobles de Qualité du Sud-Est du Bassin Parisien*, unpublished university thesis, Paris, 1981.

APPENDIX 8

Days of Frost, 1963–80

Year	April	May	April and May	Yield	Quality
1973	13	1	14	64,294 hls	Quite good
1976	9	3	12	52 hl/ha	Good
1979	6	4	10	77 hl/ha	Good
1969	9	1	10	28 hl/ha	Excellent
1965	6	3	9	22,496 hls	Very poor
1968	6	3	9	21,181 hls	Poor
1980	7	2	9	53 hl/ha	Average
1974	8	1	9	49 hl/ha	Below average
1977	9	0	9	37 hl/ha	Below average
1978	9	0	9	34 hl/ha	Excellent
1975	9	0	9	53 hl/ha	Excellent
1967	6	2	8	25,668 hls	Good
1971	7	1	8	23,527 hls	Excellent
1970	8	0	8	74,498 hls?	Good
1963	3	3	6	30,033 hls	Poor
1964	4	0	4	24,041 hls	Very good
1966	4	0	4	45 hl/ha	Good
1972	1	2	3	35,056 hls	Disastrous

It is impossible to give an average yield per hectare for every year, as the area of production is not always known. The vintages of 1966 and 1970 were considered very large at the time.

APPENDIX 9

Members of the Co-operative, La Chablisienne

BEINES
Léon Albar
Jacques Blanvillain
Chambre d'Agriculture d'Auxerre
Jean Claude Dauvissat
Fernand Joussot
Paul Joussot
Rémy Lefort
GAEC Michaut Frères
Gérard Patrice
Georgette Robin
Roger Roblot
André Villain
Roger Zozime

BÉRU
Olympe Laventureux
André Pagnier
Maurice Pagnier

CHABLIS
Félix Beau
Jean Bègue
GAEC du Domaine du Château de Grenouilles
Robert Fèvre
Jean Pierre Gouailhardou
André Raimond
Henri Robin
Michel Robin
Paul Robin
Robin Jules Simon
Michelle and Jean Claude Soupe

CHEMILLY
Christian Cherbuy
Georges Détollé
Henri Détollé
Maurice Détollé
Albert Durand

Edmond Kaczmar
Bernard Lavaud
Daniel Lompré
René Lompré
Paul Martin
Roger Mathieu
Edmond Nicolle
GAEC du Patos
Christian Race
Jacques Race
Monique Race

CHICHÉE
Jean Gasser
Michel Michaut
René Michaut
Paul Robin
Jean Robin

COURGIS
Daniel Adine
Marc Adine
Maurice Adine
Joseph Aubron
Pierre Barbier
Gabriel Bouc
Jacques Bouc
Marie Louise Bernard
Bernard Cathelin
Jean Pierre Chapotin
Philibert Chapotin
Alfred Ducastelle
Jean Robert Dufour
Robert Dufour
André Dupré
Gilbert Dupré
Jacques Foulley
Philippe Foulley

Michel George
Roger George
Héritiers Mineur
Odette Jacque Mineur
Roger Landais
Raymond Maingonnat
Françoise Quittot
Gilbert Quittot
André Race
Gaston Race
Gilbert Race
Marcel Race
Roland Race
Daniel Rétif
Pierre Rétif
Yves Valluet
René Vitteaux

FLEYS
Henri Barraud
Cécile Chamon
Guy Collon
Alain Couperot
Eugène Couperot
Jean Couperot
Jean Louis Couperot
Robert Couperot
Lionel Dauvissat
Bernard Fournillon
Robert Rousseau
Carmen Vaillier

FONTENAY-PRÉS-CHABLIS
Philippe Brousseau
Pierre and Robert Carré
Bernard de Oliveira
GAEC de Oliveira, Père et Fils
Guy Dupas
Henri Dupas
GAEC Fèvre Frères
André Lecestre
George Mathieu
Charles Moreau

Fernand Mothe
Ulysse Porcheron
Jean Pierre Rousseau
Pierre Rousseau
Antoine Ventura
José Ventura
Michel Vrignaud

FYÉ
Jean Marie Bonnet
Marcel Bonnet
Maurice Bonnet
Antoine Chapuis
Michel Dauvissat
André Fèvre
Régis Fèvre
René Fèvre
Charles Goutant
André Lanier
Eliane Raoult
Charles Rapet
André Renaud
André Vuillaume
Bernard Dampt

LA CHAPELLE VAUPELTEIGNE
Guy Alexandre
Guy Aligon
Alain Crochot
Armand Crochot
René Defert
Alfred Foynat
Pierre Foynat
René Jolly
Robert Jolly
Vve André Lhoste
Jean Claude Lhoste
Maurice Lhoste
Pierre Paulay
Henri Tremblay
Patrick Thouverey
Vve Daniel Tupinier
Marcel Tupinier

LIGNORELLES
Jean Beaufumé
Henri Crochot
Christiane Fassier
Christine Gallois
Marcellin Gallois
Francis Pautré
GAEC Pautré, Père et Fils
Evelyne Perrot
Jean Claude Tremblay
Suzanne Tremblay

MALIGNY
Jacques Gautheron
Maurice Gautheron
Paul Jolly
Paul Jossot
Pierre Jossot
Paul Laroche
Louis Lorot

MILLY
Jean Bourcey
Roland Bourcey
Pierre Céléstin
Jacques Jannet
Jean Jannet
Daniel and Ginette Perrot
Fernand Peigné
Robert Peigné
Georges Roblot
Pierre Villetard
Raoul Villetard

POILLY–SUR–SEREIN
Claude Malaquin
Jacques Moreau

POINCHY
Marcel Cottenot
Georges Crochot
Michel Duchemin
Michel Jannet
Félix Mothère
Marthe Roblot
Louis Simonot
René Simonot

PRÉHY
Théodore Wengier
GAEC des Reugnis

VILLY
Raymond Bachelier
Roger Bachelier
Jean Couturat
Gaston Lecuillier
Pierre Pigé
Daniel Poitout

VIVIERS
Jean Balacey
Jean Luc Balacey
Gérard Grandjean

APPENDIX 10

Dates of the 'Bans de Vendange' in the Auxerrois and Chablisien

The dates for the years 1700–1893 have been taken from a chart in the possession of Serge Hugot at Coulanges-la-Vineuse.

1700	10 October	1734	27 September	1769	9 October
1701	27 September	1735	15 October	1770	15 October
1702	20 September	1736	28 September	1771	9 October
1703	28 September	1737	1 October	1772	5 October
1704	15 September	1738	8 October	1773	7 October
1705	5 October	1739	1 October	1774	3 October
1706	16 September	1740	20 October	1775	4 October
1707	28 September	1741	28 September	1776	14 October
1708	28 September	1742	16 October	1777	16 October
1709	No vintage; vines frozen	1743	3 October	1778	5 October
		1744	12 October	1779	27 September
1710	30 September	1745	11 October	1780	2 October
1711	No information	1746	10 October	1781	24 September
1712	30 September	1747	2 October	1782	14 October
1713	11 October	1748	3 October	1783	29 September
1714	1 October	1749	1 October	1784	20 September
1715	30 September	1750	1 October	1785	3 October
1716	30 September	1751	13 October	1786	16 October
1717	6 October	1752	9 October	1787	15 October
1718	19 September	1753	3 October	1788	22 September
1719	22 September	1754	14 October	1789	13 October
1720	7 October	1755	24 September	1790	7 October
1721	7 October	1756	13 October	1791	3 October
1722	30 September	1757	3 October	1792	9 October
1723	23 September	1758	27 September	1793	8 October
1724	2 October	1759	1 October	1794	15 September
1725	23 October	1760	29 September	1795	5 October
1726	15 September	1761	27 September	1796	10 October
1727	22 September	1762	20 September	1797	8 October
1728	22 September	1763	17 October	1798	24 September
1729	5 October	1764	3 October	1799	28 September
1730	9 October	1765	7 October	1800	2 October
1731	1 October	1766	13 October	1801	6 October
1732	8 October	1767	26 October	1802	25 September
1733	29 September	1768	3 October	1803	4 October

1804	1 October	1834	22 September	1864	28 September
1805	21 October	1835	8 October	1865	14 September
1806	28 September	1836	4 October	1866	3 October
1807	27 September	1837	9 October	1867	30 September
1808	3 October	1838	11 October	1868	14 September
1809	15 October	1839	30 September	1869	27 September
1810	8 October	1840	28 September	1870	15 September
1811	19 September	1841	4 October	1871	2 October
1812	15 October	1842	22 September	1872	28 September
1813	14 October	1843	16 October	1873	6 October
1814	13 October	1844	26 September	1874	17 September
1815	30 October	1845	13 October	1875	27 September
1816	24 October	1846	13 September	1876	5 October
1817	12 October	1847	4 October	1877	1 October
1818	28 September	1848	2 October	1878	3 October
1819	4 October	1849	1 October	1879	19 October
1820	12 October	1850	9 October	1880	25 September
1821	18 October	1851	8 October	1881	28 September
1822	5 September	1852	30 September	1882	2 October
1823	16 October	1853	10 October	1883	8 October
1824	14 October	1854	12 October	1884	4 October
1825	24 September	1855	8 October	1885	1 October
1826	2 October	1856	6 October	1886	4 October
1827	1 October	1857	22 September	1887	29 September
1828	6 October	1858	23 September	1888	11 October
1829	12 October	1859	20 September	1889	26 September
1830	30 September	1860	15 October	1890	4 October
1831	29 September	1861	30 September	1891	8 October
1832	8 October	1862	25 September	1892	26 September
1833	30 September	1863	1 October	1893	7 October

Ironically, most of the dates for this century are impossible to obtain from an authoritative source. The exceptions are the following, supplied by the INAO in Dijon.

1982	20 September	1979	5 October	1976	15 September
1981	2 October	1978	10 October	1974	30 September
1980	14 October	1977	15 October	1969	10 October

BIBLIOGRAPHY

Books

Warner Allen, *The Romance of Wine*, London, 1931

Maynard A. Amerine et al. *The Technology of Wine Making*, Westport, Connecticut, AVI Publishing, 1980

John Arlott and Christopher Fielden, *Burgundy, Vines and Wines*, London, Davis-Poynter, 1976

Charles Albert d'Arnoux, *Dissertation sur la situation de Bourgogne*, London, 1728

Philip Miller, trans., *The Gardener's Dictionary*, London, 1733

Félix Benoit and Henry Clos-Jouve, *La Bourgogne insolite et gourmande*, Solarama, 1976

Charles Walter Berry, *In Search of Wine, A Tour of the Vineyards of France*, London, 1935

Louis Bro, *Chablis, Porte d'Or de la Bourgogne*, Paris, 1959

Jean Alexandre Cavoleau, *Oenologie Française*, Paris, 1827

Claude Courtepée, *Histoire Abrégée du Duché de Bourgogne*, Dijon, 1777

Roger Dion, *Histoire de la Vigne et du Vin en France des Origines au XIX Siècle*, Paris, Flammarion, 1959

Pierre-Marie Doutrelant, *Les Bons Vins et les Autres*, Paris, Edition du Seuil, 1976

Robert Druitt, *Report on Cheap Wines*, Edinburgh, 1865

J. Duband, *Histoire de Chablis*, Sens, 1852

William Fèvre, *Les Vrais Chablis et les Autres*, Colmar, 1978

Pierre Forgeot, *Pélérinage aux sources de Bourgogne*, Colmar, 1971

Pierre Galet, *Cépages et Vignobles de France*, Montpelier, 1958

Gérard Jack Gilbank, *Les Vignobles de Qualité du Sud-Est du Bassin Parisien*, unpublished university thesis, Paris, 1981

Françoise Grivot, *Le Commerce des Vins de Bourgogne*, Paris, 1962

Jules Guyot, *Etudes des Vignobles de France*, Paris, 1868

Anthony Hanson, *Burgundy*, London, Faber, 1982

Evelyn M. Hatch, *Burgundy Past and Present*, London, Methuen, 1927

Louis Jacquelin and René Poulain, *Vignes et Vins de France*, Paris, Flammarion, 1960

Paul Jamain, with Georges Bellair and Claude Moreau, *La Vigne et Le Vin*, Paris, Doin, 1901, vol. II, *Atlas Vinicole* (maps by Hausermann)

André Jullien, *Topographie des Vins de France*, Paris, 1816; 2nd ed. (*Topographie de Tous les Vignobles Connus*), Paris, 1822

Alexis Lichine, *The Wines of France*, London, Cassell, 1952

Dr McBride, *General Instructions for the Choice of Wines and Spirituous Liquors*, London, 1793

The Wines of Chablis

Monographie Agricole de l'Yonne, 1924

Denis Morris, *The French Vineyards*, London, 1958

P. Morton Shand, rev. and ed. Cyril Ray, *A Book of French Wines*, Harmondsworth, Penguin, 1968

Alexandre Odart, *Ampelographie Universelle*, Paris, 1874

Albert Pic, *Le Vignoble de Chablis*, Paris, 1935

Pierre Poupon and Pierre Forgeot, *Les Vins de Bourgogne*, 8th ed., Vendôme, Presses Universitaires de France, 1977

Cyrus Redding, *A History and Description of Modern Wines*, London, Whittaker, Treacher and Arnot, 1833

Victor Rendu, *Ampelographie Française*, Paris, 1857

Grimod de la Reynière, *Journal des Gourmands et des Belles*, Vol. IV, 1807

Eugène Rousseaux and Georges Chappaz, *Etude sur le Vignoble de Chablis*, Nancy, 1904

André Simon, *The Blood of the Grape, the Wine Trade Text Book*, London, 1920

André Simon, *History of the Wine Trade in England*, London 1905/6

Vintagewise, 3rd ed., London, Michael Joseph, 1946

Charles Tovey, *Wine and Wine Countries*, London, 1877

William Younger, *Gods, Wine and Men*, London, Michael Joseph, 1968

Articles

Michel Bettane, 'Attention! Un Chablis peut cacher un autre', *Revue du Vin de France*, no. 286, 1981

Pierre Brejoux, 'Le Chablis', *Revue du Vin de France*, July 1976

Martin Forde, 'Chablis; The Law of the Market', *Wine & Spirit*, October 1981

Bill Jekel, 'Factors for Fine Wine', *Decanter*, August 1982

GLOSSARY AND LIST OF ABBREVIATIONS

climat   A named vineyard site.

commissionaire   Broker: a go-between for grower and *négociant*.

courtier   The same as a *commissionaire*; the more commonly used of the two terms.

cuvé   Vat.

cuverie   Cellar containing vats.

domaine   Estate.

guyot   Method of pruning; it may be single or double, with one or two branches respectively.

élevage   The 'rearing', or 'bringing up', of the wine.

feuillette   Traditional Chablis barrel, with a capacity of 132 litres. Although wine is no longer sold in a *feuillette*, prices are still reckoned in this unit.

foudre   Large wooden barrel.

fouloir   Machine in which the grapes are crushed.

fût   Small wooden barrel.

intronisation   Ceremony of introduction to a wine brotherhood.

moelleux   Soft and rich, but not sweet.

passage au froid   Process of freezing the wine for a short period in order to precipitate the tartrate crystals, so that these can be filtered out of the wine.

plantes nobles   Noble grape varieties. These are obligatory for the production of *appellation contrôlée* wines, in contrast with the many high-yielding hybrid grape varieties (planted after the phylloxera outbreak) which are not allowed for *appellation contrôlée* wines.

negociant éleveur   Négociant who deals in wine. He may or may not own vineyards, but he does buy grapes, or must, or made wine from growers, which he treats and sells.

remuage   The process of turning bottles of sparkling wine so that the sediment created by the secondary fermentation falls onto the cork of the bottle and can be removed. This is done by a *remuer*.

'simple' Chablis   Chablis that is not *grand cru*, *premier cru* or Petit Chablis – in other words, the basic and largest part of the appellation. The term is used to avoid any confusion with the name of the town and the area as a whole.

sous marque   A large export house will have several labels, or *sous marques*, as well as its own name, to enable it to deal with several importers on the same market, without any clash of interest.

taille   Pruning.

tracteur enjambeur   Type of tractor designed for use in vineyards. It is high enough to straddle a row of vines.

vendangeur   Harvester who picks the grapes.

vigneron   Someone who grows grapes and makes his own wine.

viticulteur   Grower of grapes, but not a wine-maker.

vin de garde   A wine that will age, with all the necessary keeping qualities.

vin de primeur   A wine for early drinking, with no keeping qualities.

vin gris   Rosé wine.

CNAO   Comité Nationale d'Appellation d'Origine; forerunner of the INAO (qv).

CIB   Comité Interprofessionel des Vins de Bourgogne; it includes Chablis.

GAEC   Groupement Agricole d'Exploitation en Commun. A father with sons will often form a GAEC to run the family vineyards.

INAO   Institut d'Appellation d'Origine.

SAFER   Société d'Amenagement Foncier d'Etablissement Rural: the organization responsible for the development of rural France.

SICAVA   Société d'Intérêt Collectif Agricole du Vignoble Auxerrois; it produces Crémant de Bourgogne at Bailly on a collective basis.

VDQS   Vin Délimité de Qualité Supérieur: the category below *appellation contrôlée*. Sauvignon de Saint Bris is the only VDQS wine produced in the Yonne.

INDEX
Figures in *italics* refer to illustrations